Mindfulness & Family

SIMPLE STEPS OF 'WORKING WITH THE MIND'
FOR EVERYDAY AND FAMILY LIFE

WORKING WITH THE MIND SERIES

Working With The Mind Publishing
WWTM.ORG/PUBLICATIONS
978-1-8383176-0-7
We do not warrant or make any representations regarding the use or
the results of the use of the exercises in this book, supporting mate-
rials, or on our website site in terms of their correctness, accuracy,
timeliness, reliability or otherwise. Mindfulness is a personal practice, and if you have any concerns about it you can contact us further
via our website, or social media group. All the titles in the working
with the mind series support the ongoing development of community mindfulness programmes

Author's note

What is working with the mind? Like any process for understanding and experiencing ourselves and our reactions to the world around us, this can be thought of as like the spread of Information Technology (IT). Not that long ago in the grand scheme of things, before computers were basic life tools for schools, homes and businesses, not everyone could do simple stuff with basic computing technology, and many still cannot. The skill of using computers to process and access information, make documents, compile reports and communicate with each other, weren't as commonplace as they are now. There were IT consultants teaching people how to do it, showing pupils, students, employers and employees the how and the why (or the process and benefits) of using IT. Working with the mind is similar because right now there are people working in schools, communities, businesses and various other environments, who are introducing the process of greater awareness of the mind and the positive implications this offers. Today's world emphasises the importance of dealing with stress, anxiety and depression – some of the most significant health concerns of our time that impact all areas of life, yet we don't all have the skills to manage these things. All things 'of the mind' are still just a little new for many people, seemingly unobtainable and not something practical we can engage with. Much like the wave of IT consultants showing people how and why to use a computer, there is currently an increasing trend in the support available to help us actually implement strategies for working with the mind, towards whatever benefit and improvement may be applicable to us. Martial arts, yoga, meditation, spiritual and religious practices and whole hosts of other programmes and exercises are founded upon similar principles that we introduce in this book through the Working With The Mind programme.

This generation's awareness of mental health and psychological well-being is far greater than ever before, merely as a natural effect of modern-day living and the amount of information and conflicting duties and responsibilities present in life today. We may live longer and have better access to finances and other resources than ever before in the history of humanity but we are not necessarily all that happier, healthier or free from suffering because of it. We all know stress, anxiety and depression, have experienced these or know someone who does; and that it's supposed to be OK to talk to people about them. However, how many of us know someone who can do something practical about them when they arise? These represent only some examples, and actually all our states of mind, emotions, areas of challenge and difficulty we face in life other than mental health, stem from the mind too. By addressing the mind so too, can we then take steps to transform some of the root causes of mental health difficulties and suffering we find there. The implications and impacts of negative states of mind and the precursors to the psychological states we experience in the mind are wide-reaching. Within the family setting this influences how we interact with each other: how prepared we are to deal with our own mind; how effectively we can parent our kids or how well we can put up with our parents telling us what to do; how we may look at the support of our parents during the end-of-life stages and even through the natural conflicts we experience; and when our families break down or family members suffer. How we refer to these in the mind has an impact on all these aspects, and on how affected we become by states of mind and emotions connected to these experiences.

Progressively larger proportions of our culture are looking for strategies to strengthen and develop the mind, in much the same way as we've had a former focus on developing our understanding and experience of improving the body and our physical selves for a better experience of life. The how and why of working with the mind, of transforming the way we look at and engage with the difficulties and challenges inherent in the mind, is one of the next most fundamental of human endeavours. Until most people had the awareness of IT and its use, there wasn't much desire or need for it. Now, try doing any job, contacting any person or engaging in any learning without using such technology. Collectively we were unaware of the shift until we realised that we are personally worse off if we are unable to use these skills – we tend not to see such change until a 'tipping point' occurs before we sit up and take note. Such is the way that awareness shifts, and that happens gradually, person by person. Most certainly, in today's world we are worse off for not having some awareness of, and heightened ability to take account of and alter our states of mind.

The World Health Organisation states that "one in four people in the world will be affected by mental or neurological disorders at some point in their lives, placing mental disorders among the leading causes of ill-health and disability worldwide"[1]. For a world where an estimated 970 million people worldwide had (any) mental disorder[2] just a few years before this book was published, the value of information and support on working with the mind seems as valid and beneficial now as was the need for IT consultants only a few decades ago. Our support services for matters of the mind and mental health are woefully behind those we have available to care for our physical health. This is because it is only recently in more mainstream public opinion, scientific research and health care terms that we have begun to look at the role of the mind more openly and in earnest.

As far back as when early medicine was advancing, there was a distinct separation of body and mind[3]. Health and well-being were considered to be all about the body, and the mind, soul or spirit was thought of as entirely separate and left to the realms of the church or philosophers. Today, through growing understanding, increasing research and more support out there to open up receptivity to the mind a little, we see that all things are of the mind. We see that we cannot develop our healthcare without looking at the mind[4], and we can't support adults and children to learn to deal with difficulty faced in life without working with the mind in some way. The change from viewing all things of the mind as new-age, and all

meditative, self-reflective and mindfulness-based practices as slightly woolly, is quickly becoming outdated. We
often simply just don't see the change coming.

There are guided exercises in all the books in the
Working With The Mind series, and these are designed to
be accessible to all of us regardless of how experienced
we are in awareness training. However, self-guided practice can be hard to start out with so, to support this as
much as possible, there is an online Working With The
Mind community you can join for other free support and
services, and there are free guided audio exercises available with this book. Bridging the gap between whatever
our current outlook and understanding is, and an in-depth
experience of using these exercises and tools, is vital
to the positive outcomes from working with the mind.
There may be a natural resistance to some of the process
of doing this, for most of us at one point or other when
embarking on this kind of learning and self-development.
We will come up against this time and time again, so noticing the onset of this is extremely useful in everyday and
family life!

It's key to get as much understanding and experience of
the different practical exercises involved as possible, and
of what support they can provide for us individually and as
families. The resulting benefits and experiential learning
we gain from this, help to bolster the understanding we
can get from thinking, reading and talking about the process. It's very easy to overlook the simplicity of the idea of
looking at, and working with the mind, because it seems
so unobtainable or there is some expectation that it will
get in the way of normal life. This series of books attempts

to lay out a simple step-by-step process to follow, which builds our understanding and experience of developing a greater mindful outlook. Follow these steps as openly as you can (see **Appendix 3) The steps of working with the mind** for all the steps), and if you find some resistance to or difficulty with what is discussed, remember that's OK and just be aware of this. The understanding and experience gained from this reading must be yours, and some of the ideas and principles contained in this book may not resonate with you according to how you are experiencing life at the moment. We certainly do not need to become any sort of mindfulness master, or to retreat from life to the monastery to realise a significant benefit for ourselves and our family life. So, should the content present a challenge, don't fear; there's no need for a radical overhaul of who we are and how we see the world! By reading this book, and with continued guidance, we'll find that some of these ideas really do grow our resilience through life's ebb and flow, help change the way we see ourselves, and enable us to more openly appreciate and support our families. For those of us who are time-strapped, this process need only start with 10 minutes here and there, as we'll see in some of research discussed later in the book. There is also a final chapter of the book, which acts as a shortened version or summary of the content covered (other than the guided exercises included). This 'book in brief' chapter will hopefully make it easier to digest, and maximise retention of the key points covered (see Chapter 10). It has been found that those who read books for 30 minutes daily lived an average of 23 months longer than non-readers or magazine readers[5], so an abbreviated version of working with the mind books may also help us read more regularly and live a little longer – so consider the final chapter a gift!

Proceeds from all the books in this series support those served through mindfulness-based community programmes, so thanks to all who have made this book possible – from those who have participated in the community projects that formed and developed the steps of the Working With The Mind programme, to those who supported the development of the social enterprise and these books in so many ways, including those who agreed to answer some questions on the family life they live and the challenges presented there, those who volunteered time and effort to give feedback on the book, our volunteer proof-reader, content designer, as well as the professionals involved in editing, designing and generally making the book possible. Whilst reading this if there is an interest in seeking further ideas, information or support, the **Appendix** provides a guide to more resources and free content, as well as more in-depth services that are available. For those of us whose family difficulties are significant, ongoing, and get the better of us time and time again, and for all of us living with the ongoing challenges of life and our family situations, may this book provide some relief and support. May we all experience freedom from this suffering and its root causes through a developed ability to see this challenge in the most positive light we can.

Contents

Prologue

orking with the mind (or WWTM) is a programme adapted from community mindfulness-based initiatives, established and run through UK social enterprise, which now are supported by proceeds from WWTM courses, services, products and publications. More information is available online at WWTM.ORG. In 2020, all the programmes run in various community groups were reviewed, each ending in fantastic results using only a compilation of the steps represented in this book. Building our own understanding and experience of the principles covered in the exercises in this series, has never been more accessible. Bridging that gap between the parts of the mind that we usually remain unaware and inattentive of, and a space of heightened awareness, is remarkably helpful in life. During the book we will review much of the research out there to support the understanding of this as much as possible, and there are also 3 exercise chapters to help guide our own experience of this.

As individuals we have increasingly complicated lives, and simple concepts are easily overlooked, or cast aside and ignored completely. This book aims to provide the reader with a simple understanding and experience, ot how to develop a greater awareness and attention, then use this to more clearly see how to get the most out of every day and family life (including how to manage the inevitable challenges involved). Working with the mind is nothing more complex than a continued developing of our use of attention and awareness to greater effect in life. We will explore how to do this, and discuss what may be noticed and how to adapt our approaches along the way. Through establishing a focus on compassionate, grateful and positive means we transform the mind, and later in this book we will introduce the process of doing this for the benefit of ourselves and our family.

Family means different things to different people, and there is no standard or norm by which we can (or should) measure a family. There is certainly nothing more helpful we can do to support and grow our family, to navigate the inevitable difficulty this entails along the way, than to improve ourselves. The intended focus of this book is specifically on using the exercises and ideas introduced towards this end. Working with the mind is about taking stock of ourselves and our mind, then doing the work of repairing, developing and maintaining – something we all have the choice to ignore or to engage in, but not that we all have the competency to do as the skills involved can appear elusive. Healthy, wholesome relationships with ourselves and our loved ones may seem simple, but family is actually pretty hard. In fact, raising children, nurturing our relationships with our partners, parents and siblings are some of the most demanding tasks we can bring ourselves to in life. With regard to family life, working with the mind is about using tools, skills, learning, information and support to understand and experience our own states of mind more completely, and how these impact on the family around us. Using this we can engage with some of the difficulty we normally face within family life, becoming gradually more able to influence and change our immediate space of awareness. We constantly have to look through the eyes of others within families, even give more of ourselves than we may be receiving from others at times, and we can often find time for ourselves is restricted. To subdue perhaps even our own desires and preferences by prioritising another duty or responsibility, can involve lots of emotional energy and we often have little awareness of managing this effectively. Through reading this book we gain a clearer insight into making sure that our impact on family, and the effect our family has on us, are as positive and productive as possible. By using the principles in this book, we come progressively to notice all those frames of mind, and aspects of ourselves that contribute to negative experience in our life and how to mitigate any influences from this for ourselves and those around us in the family. This is a very individual and personal process, which we adapt naturally according to our needs as we progress. Thankfully there's no need to turn away from what makes us who we are, and the tools provided here are accessible and adaptable to all backgrounds and walks of life. Follow the steps as they're laid out, and these can then be easily changed to suit our specific routines once we're familiar with them.

Just by continually striving to be the best version of ourselves we can bring ourselves to be within our specific family unit, involves a lot of introspection and self-awareness – some of the most challenging things we can do. Where we choose to do this well it can be a real eye-opening experience, one where we can learn a lot about ourselves as individuals and as a population. It's fundamental to navigate changes in life; so that we can honour and support the development of others in our family, and be as positive a part of it as we can. Allowing ourselves the brief time to reflect on this is sorely needed for today's world, where we have tended to forget that our strength as individuals, families and communities doesn't come from hardening ourselves to or disassociating from daily tasks. Opening up in mind and heart to whatever is present, is strength beyond that which is needed to be as great an individual person and family member as we need to be, whatever our role and position in life.

Being open-minded is certainly becoming less of a taboo to exercise, and has measurable and diverse effects in areas from health and wellbeing to interracial attitudes[1] and responses to sexuality[2]. It's slowly becoming easier to be more open-minded, where today we have more available, accessible and affordable ways of learning how to work with the mind towards improved outcomes for ourselves individually and collectively. To do so in the context of family, an awareness of our self and how we fit into and influence the family unit is powerful. There is no end to the potential changes and development in society and civilisation, technologically and scientifically which affect the way we live family life today. In this world, if we are not careful, much of family life is over-shadowed by external influences from the world at large. Ostensibly there's nothing wrong with this, yet we need to take some care and attention to note what forms and conditions our values, intentions, ambitions, beliefs and regular habits. Essentially, this forms us – who we are and what we do – right down to the level of how we think, speak and act.

It is fair to suggest that for many of us this is influenced far more significantly by influences from without than those from within. Our attention is on anything but the here-and-now, present moment experience of being alive. Noticing what is going on in the body, mind, and experience of now is in the background of awareness – while the foreground is busily engaged in forever reacting to what's going on. Usually this is through thinking and worrying about many aspects of life, or building the emotional story attached to and arising from it. Much of this is based on what we think and feel about what happens to us in the present, and not the present just as itself as it is, without our filter of perception. What occurs is largely random, or at least immediately beyond us to influence and control, so to take account of it we internalise this experience of life moment-by-moment. Here we have some control of the process of what happens to us in life, a subtle way of filtering information and sensory impulses to help structure reality into manageable chunks. By these means we become conscious of our individual way of perceiving reality, rather than simply remaining conscious of our reality itself. It may seem less boring, challenging or annoying to be of the moment than in it perhaps, but developing greater awareness of the process of focusing our attention instead of allowing what's around us to determine what we notice, is far more powerful.

The difficulty and challenge within our families, is

genuinely caused less often than we think by the family life itself and what goes on – it's the commotion made in the mind as we observe life with merely fractured attention and individual perspective which really causes difficulties. Family duties, responsibilities and life is something our minds can make a real mess of, especially as we are largely conscious of our perception of it rather than simply of it by itself as it arises and passes each moment. Now we are going to progressively delve into how to develop a resilience to deal with this process, and a proactive way of ensuring that when we're caught up in how we feel and think about what is going on, we can shift perspective back to the frame of mind of just being present, and aware of what's going on in life. With remarkably little time and practice we will come to see the value of this for ourselves, if we haven't already to some degree. However, before starting the book, here are some statements to begin with:

Birth is strange, although we don't seem to remember it – first we were not and then we were. It's an unusual development going from nothing to something!

Developing references as a baby involves lots of repetition, after all if there's nothing in the mind at all, it needs to be filled doesn't it?

Being a small child, and conforming to the will of the household's responsible adult(s) is a challenge.

Managing the expectations of our parent(s), whilst coming to a realisation of our own self and desires can be tricky.

Surviving our own growth, adolescence and the impact of our upbringing in a relatively unscathed manner is rare.

Being a young adult is complicated, with decisions, emotions and independence being quite as restrictive as the constraints of the family we have painstakingly severed ourselves from.

Starting our own family is quite an ordeal and to balance the needs of those we end up surrounded by, while making sure we also have enough energy, money and time to ourselves, is an ongoing juggling act.

Being a parent and a husband, wife, or partner is hard; and being a single parent is an on-going trial.

Having to do lots of things for our kids can feel like tasks that continue forever, such as explaining the effect of things and establishing healthy boundaries. Do we sometimes end up doing more harm as we do this?

Dealing with conflict, trauma, grief and the challenge of family is not something we often feel prepared for.

Growing older is sometimes tiring and although our naps are socially acceptable, our wisdom is only as valid as the ears it falls on, and in today's world most families keep too busy to hear much of it.

Death in the family seems strange, unnatural and can evoke a lot of fear and apprehension before it's possible for us to arrive at joy and appreciation for the lives around us – including those which have ended.

Actually these statements could continue ad infinitum, but the point is only to bear in mind when you read through this book that family is one of the most fundamental of human needs and endeavours. This is not an insignificant journey we take, and by choice or by default our very civilisation is built on how we continually bring about the next generations as families. Thinking about this, a greater awareness of how to navigate family life is invaluable, especially when trying to come to grips with the difficulties of family life. The development and self-realisation that we go through in order to be able to support each other, and our own self in this regard, is pretty important. We're actually not all great people, and naturally don't want to have to give away more of ourselves then we get back. Therefore, realising how to move this state of mind to a space of being willing and able can be rather tricky. For some it can be really difficult if there are many experiences leaving us predisposed quite naturally towards being self-centred, or towards more downward-spiralling beliefs and values. Family can be tough on everyone involved, so consider the family outcomes where our subconscious is conditioned to be unloving, self-centred, nasty, indifferent or aggressive – what might the impacts on family life and future generations be? This book is not meant to tell us how to live our life, or what our family dynamic should and could be, simply to point to a few ideas and guide some experiences that will be all the more helpful for us whatever our current understanding and experience of family life may be.

Attention and awareness

We are what we repeatedly do.

Excellence then is not an act, but a habit.

*E*very one of us gets faced with challenges, both physical and mental, at different points or particular junctures of our lives. Feelings of sadness, frustration, lack of motivation, depression and physical concerns cannot be ignored and need to be attended to. Yet all of us are experts at looking the other way!

We plough through these experiences as they arise, just to get through them and move on, rarely considering how or why they come about at all. We don't see the triggers that build up to create a negative experience of a situation, and we don't reflect on conflict or strengthen the process of easing and recovering from this. All these things that impact upon us at a personal level, also affect the family unit that we're part of. Learning to be more aware of these triggers, and to work with our attention for more positive outcomes as challenging situations arise, is key to mitigating harmful effects of the unchecked difficulties we face.

In essence, we can change our experience of the present moment, no matter how challenging or upsetting it may be, by using our attention more creatively. Such awareness and attention also enables us to take our family unit into account as a whole, towards achieving a greater appreciation and understanding of the interactions, both positive and negative that we have with family members. All those things left out of our immediate awareness, relegated to the subconscious realm of the mind outside our usual focus, will inevitably cause more harm if left there unattended to while we get on with life and dealing with the status quo.

We try to avoid the unpleasantness of challenge, and

this avoidance is actually far more life-limiting – often without our knowing why. When we haven't allowed ourselves to go through the process of dealing with and opening up to negativity, the challenges and difficulties faced are all the more overwhelming. This is true on the purely individual level, and also as a family. Viewing these things in the clear light of mindful observation, rather than through the perspective of emotional, reactive and more immediate involvement, is a simple, effective way of facing life rather than running from it or blindly running through it.

This is something that we're all caught up in doing far too often. However, working more openly with the mind is an effective process that has been shown to help in improving our mental and general health and well-being[1]. It can be a fascinating process and, in coming to develop our understanding and experience of our mind, we realise a greater self-awareness.

Many aspects of ourselves that we assume are rigid, fixed and true, are suddenly more flexible and can be adapted and considered in new and empowering ways. Theory and understanding in the scientific community, through social psychology and neuroscience for example, has made an investigation into the realms of working with the mind much more accessible over the last couple of decades. Things that we take for granted about humanity, our body and our mind are continually being explored further and new insights discovered – for example the way the mind reconstructs our memories. Episodic memory (of everyday events and experiences) is far more flexible than we originally assumed, and can be easily influenced by our emotions at the time of the event or experience, and again at the time of remembering the event. The mind truly is a wonderful thing, and a greater understanding of it is a powerful tool to get the best from ourselves and our family experience.

Throughout this book, we will learn about different ideas, techniques and principles of mindfulness-based exercises, as part of the 'working with the mind pro-gramme'. In this chapter we will be introducing the funda-mental principles of mindfulness practice as our starting point: these are *attention and awareness*.

We all think we know how to pay attention to some-thing, but when that something is perhaps boring or a little uncomfortable, applying this attention can seem count-er-intuitive. For example, how we have negatively reacted to a family member, or struggled to confront negativity in our own mind-set – these kinds of things can feel tricky to actually pay any attention to right from the outset. Yet attention paid to these aspects of ourselves offers a won-derful opportunity for self-development.

Most people have a surprisingly low attention span overall, arguably something that is further exacerbated by day-to-day life in the modern, digitised world[2]. Our attention lasts only as long as it can, until the next atten-tion-worthy thing, then we start focusing on something else. It's very natural for the mind to wander and focus briefly on different things around us, feelings or memo-ries, and for different thoughts to keep crossing our mind in a short span of time. It becomes almost unnatural for our attention to linger on any one thing for too long; it's almost as if we begin to see too much of our own inherent self for our liking. When we pay attention to what we can become aware of, whether they are feelings, memories, thoughts or the mindful exercises we'll come to, this can have a positive effect on our life with regard to emotions, behaviour, and other habitual ways we live our lives.

Our ability to give time and attention to those things that can be uncomfortable in family life begins to grow, including the conflicts, challenges, difficulties, and even in realising how our part in these may play out. Bringing our attention back to a chosen point of focus once we've noticed it wandering between the many things it naturally pays attention to, is where awareness comes into the picture. A greater awareness of where our attention habitually and naturally goes is fascinating, although this insight may not seem as such when our attention is on something frustrating, annoying or uncomfortable! Lots of things happen in life that we don't pay deliberate attention to, and much of life that is happening on autopilot is outside of our awareness a lot of the time – often to some detrimental, or less than constructive outcomes. This awareness and attention form the first two significant steps in working with the mind, and we'll build on these ideas throughout the book as we progress (see **Appendix 3: The steps of working with the mind**).

There is no need to beat ourselves up internally, or to feel bad about a fleeting attention span because as we'll come to see, this is perfectly natural. What we're engaged with here is limiting, or reversing any harm that this can cause – or already has caused. Once we become aware that our attention jumps about so much, we can make a mental note of this, and bring our attention back to a

chosen point of focus. This is all that mindfulness practice itself actually boils down to, in the most fundamental
sense. The purpose of understanding and experiencing
this mindful state of mind is to become more aware of our
cycles and patterns of thoughts, feelings, and subsequent
reactions. We see where our attention goes, the habits
and characteristics this builds, and the effects these have
on ourselves and others. Contrary to common thought[3],
the practice of mindfulness does not require us to stop
these thoughts, feelings and reactions in any way, or to
push them out of our mind and experience of life.

Whatever arises can be observed with an open mind,
by gently bringing our attention back to a chosen point
of focus whilst observing when our habitual, negative
or limiting reactions start to unfold. We may have a very
short span of attention when we start practising such an
awareness, but as we try different activities and gain further understanding and experience, we will become more
competent at observing whatever arises. By establishing awareness of where our attention is, even where this
involves staying with something quite difficult or challenging, we have the option of using and directing attention. We'll come to our own understanding and experience
of the benefits of this and, perhaps, come to appreciate it
as quite a valuable tool to have when dealing with the challenges inherent in modern family and everyday life.

Thoughts, feelings, emotions, sensations and anything
that comes to mind when we are in the process of practising this focus and awareness, *is what it is*. We don't need
to react to these things whilst we are mindful, because
we are just observing them for what they are. Making a

mental note of what we see when our minds are engaged this way, we can see what frames of mind and reactions we habitually tend towards. How we treat others when tired, angry or upset, how we roll judgemental or negative thoughts around in the mind, and/or perhaps how inclined towards other things we are. Awareness of this is a power we seldom allow; it is like watching as a third person at a distance, then just observing the feelings, frustration, boredom, states of mind and thoughts – be they positive or negative. These come and go, and usually we don't notice this because we're engaging with them or being affected by them. Our sense of awareness of fleeting attention settles with practice and our ability to influence our own state of mind can be more significant than we may have thought about or realised before.

When we start working with the mind, it's common to notice varied thoughts zipping around, and lots of differ-ent feelings or emotional states. Often, this may seem unconnected to immediate events. It is perfectly natural for us to look externally and try to blame how we're feel-ing internally – what's happened and how we are affected by it – on something outside of ourselves. In all things and in every situation imaginable, when we develop a mindful ability to look more openly we see that most of this can-not really be blamed on anyone or anything outside of ourselves.

As we begin each exercise of attention and awareness, we may feel that we're not able to focus on one thing, be surprised by our short span of attention, or may start feeling negatively about ourselves (even if only subtly). This all stems from noticing some of the negative stuff we normally leave to subconscious awareness. Thoughts like 'this doesn't work' or 'my mind is still busy' are extremely commonplace! We don't need to suppress these thoughts; if we try to do that, they are more likely to spring back and crowd our mind again, swaying our subsequent state of mind and thoughts.

Neither do we need to necessarily believe nor act on them – they are not truth, just thoughts. We don't need to feel bad about what arises when we're observing ourselves in the present moment; thoughts are just thoughts, feelings are just feelings and sensations are just sensations. They are part of our experience of life, and are not in and of themselves what makes us who we are individually. Struggling against them tends to leave us further agitated by them, a deeply ingrained habit we come to notice about ourselves with more focused observation. Learning to let go can bring a more positive focus in life.

Think about pilots putting planes on autopilot – having engaged autopilot, they are generally not aware of what is happening in as much detail as if they were actively monitoring all the flight data consciously. Similarly, our lives can also be in an autopilot mode, where we are not aware of the present moment as life moves around us. Our attention can be divided such that we actually spend much of our time on autopilot, just going through the motions of reacting to what comes along in life, but rarely proactive, entirely aware or fully attentive. This is a natural state of mind, as our attention cannot be on too many things at once. This 'autopilot state' is more often than not our default mode, and we go through life reacting automatically, and running through many of our daily routines without having to engage our attention all that fully.

Inherently, this is a very useful state of mind, enabling our attention to be kept free to engage with what is most pressing. This is something that historically offered clear survival advantages, for example during fight or flight and in paying attention to what's immediately important for self-preservation. However, there are clear drawbacks to such a state of mind also, in that we react without specific awareness. This means that automatically our subconscious responses become our habitual, normal way of doing things in life. Left unexplored by a conscious deliberate mind, our more negative habits will proliferate here too. All of us develop character traits, intentions and thoughts that fester and can become limiting if left unchecked.

The practice of mindfulness allows us to occasionally puncture this space of continuing autopilot, and to see how many of our habits and ways of thinking, speaking, being and doing are mostly formed in a negative way when we are unaware. As we are so often conditioned without a conscious awareness of this process occurring, clearer insight into the mind offers the opportunity to consciously exert some influence over the states of mind we develop, ways in which we react and the habits we wish to consciously create in life.

This autopilot is the absorption of our attention to objects like thoughts, feelings and senses that we experience, such that the subject of wider self is forgotten. We come to identify with what's going on in life so easily because it is our immediate experience and our attention is drawn into this – determining what's going on and judging if any action is needed, if we're safe and how we feel etc. The mind is great at performing this analysis because that's what it has done naturally since time immemorial; it's a natural, habitual and hard-wired process in the brain. It occurs automatically and we don't consciously have to choose to do it, nor to actively think about it. We can think of the mind as the seat of consciousness, if that helps, from which we're aware as reality and life unfolds around us. So much information is perceived and filtered through the senses, that our attention is drawn into this object awareness, and awareness of the wider-self context – or our mind gets lost. So many sensory perceptions, thoughts, emotions and actions synchronise in each moment that consciousness is repeatedly sucked into perception – and we're aware of what's going on but there is little of ourselves at the pilot seat whilst this perceiving goes on. It's been suggested that changes in the filtering of information perceived by the senses, or 'sensory gating' as it's called, are notably different during various states and under the influence of different substances[4]. As we're repeatedly drawn into object awareness and lose self-awareness, we mistake what goes on in life for life itself, and what happens to us, and what we experience, as our actual self and not merely what is observable by oneself in the state of mind that we are in at the time.

An increased awareness of autopilot helps us to respond to situations rather than react to them automatically. This gradually shifts a *reactive* state of mind to a *responsive* one. This transformation forms the basic premise for working with the mind, and indeed, the intention behind developing a better understanding and experience of the mind. What we see in others and around us, including our own and other's language, tends to stimulate strong reactions in us. Thoughts and other objects of perception are reactive, and generally we're inclined to be easily triggered by them. The emotions, memories, associations, interpretations and further cycles of thought they give rise to, come so very naturally and habitually that we're markedly affected by them and often engage with them without having any real awareness of them. Even our decision-making processes are suggested to be the same: where we actually make up our mind before we're aware a decision has been made[5].

Accounting for all these things that so easily go unnoticed is done by becoming aware of where our attention is, and bringing back the focus to the present, whether that's the task in hand or a chosen anchor for our focused attention. We move our conscious awareness deliberately back to the self and away from awareness of what's going on in and around us. Allowing ourselves to develop in this way is probably one of the most powerful things we can do as human beings, and the benefits of being able to come back to an awareness of the present moment are numerous and varied. Ingrained and automatic habits lead to stagnation in life, and often some severe outcomes or negative associations for ourselves and our families because we wind up using the same thinking, strategies and stories about ourselves and our place in life again and again. This is the autopilot state, our automatic way of reacting to the day's events at its most detrimental. Deliberate, conscious, mindful response is needed to punctuate and break-up the subconscious, automatic reactions created in the mind in life thus far. This is essentially the beginning of the process of coming to work with the mind.

The benefits this can have are wide-reaching indeed. For the family unit, this process has been largely overlooked until more recently, where we now have a growing understanding of the mind and the importance of taking a closer look at it, and caring for it. A broken leg is set, because we see, understand and have enough experience of the limitations which could result by not healing it. When the mind impacts us similarly – as our frames of mind and reactionary habits repeated again and again start to become an interference in life – our understanding and experience of how and why this happens is less developed. The link between our mental and physical health is known, but less so about the pathways and casual effects between them[6].

As we'll explore in more detail, seeing more clearly how our reactions arise within the family setting is very useful. Where our family life, interactions with those around us and combined well-being depend on the result of our collective hearts and minds, greater awareness and attention is fundamental. Where family life is especially difficult, emotional or challenging, this is all the more valuable, and can truly transform an overwhelming and negative experience of life to something less detrimental and damaging. In coming to experience the benefits of working with the mind for improved family outcomes, this switching of mental or cognitive points of view allows us to look differently at the challenges of family life. In this way, we come to see that challenges are a natural part of family life. Whether we have immediate power to solve these challenges or not, our often negative reaction to them needn't add to the difficulty. As we develop the skill of anchoring our attention (as we'll see in Chapter 3), we come to observe ourselves in an interesting fashion.

Where our mind is occupied with the task of paying attention and by also deliberately being aware of this, we see what else arises without needing to react to it or to engage with it; we just watch it pass. Self-referential processing is a useful term to introduce here and, although this may sound quite complex, don't fret, it isn't, and it helps to illustrate this point a little further. Much of the evidence on using mindfulness, and the positive changes arising from ongoing practice of using mindfulness, touches on this idea of how we process things in the brain by reference to oneself[7]. **Figure 1.0** shows how, through continued practice of awareness and attention exercises, and using these mindful principles, the brain naturally comes to process information without such a strong connection to the self.

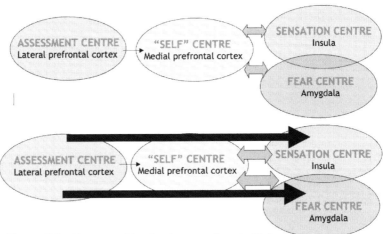

Figure 1.0 – Measured brain changes in mindfulness practitioners

The top half of the **figure** above represents the brain before engaging in mindfulness practice. Normally speaking, the parts of the brain that assess information from the senses during conflict (amygdala and insula) are less strongly connected to the assessment centre, the more rational regions of the brain (lateral prefrontal cortex). The "self-centre" of the brain has greater networks with these areas dealing with conflict in non-meditators. So, whenever conflict, a fear response, or sensations arise in the mind, it's apparently quite normal to internalise them and not to see them as connected to events outside ourselves. This results in more internal conflict, as if the situation and challenge it presents in the moment is accepted as *us* rather than as something happening *to us*. After establishing a practice of awareness and attention, shown by the lower half of **Figure 1.0**, "self-centre" connections to the insula and amygdala are weakened. Assessment centre pathways are strengthened[8], and it's more straightforward to externalise sensations and fear, resulting in a more tempered response to conflict and threat. This causes a subsequent reduction in the natural anxiety in the mind's responses. Put simply, measured changes in the brain after meditation mean we don't take things so personally, and can see situations as they are, instead of how they affect us as the individual perceiving them.

If establishing greater awareness, or working with the attention of the mind seem far-fetched or sound complicated and daunting, fear not! Because whether these are entirely new ideas, or skills we may already have worked on, the rest of the book will help to expand our current understanding *and experience of this* – whatever our background and family life may be. One of the most powerful things we can do for ourselves and our family in the world of today, is to come to an awareness of how life changes and fluctuates, because it is (and we are) never consistently in one state for long. Subsequently, our states of mind are rarely long-lived, and how we naturally react to life is often outside of our immediate awareness, especially when life is challenging. Becoming more competent at working with the mind supports us to see this naturally changing flow of things, without getting so caught-up and frustrated by it when things aren't going our way.

Becoming more competent at this has to start with realising just how unaware we are of what goes on in the mind, of our unconscious incompetence. When we start to work consciously to build on this and develop our understanding and experience of working with the mind, we quickly see what works well for us in gaining a conscious competence of these exercises using the steps we'll progress through in this book. In time, and if it's of practical assistance to us in our family life, it's fairly straightforward to arrive at a state of unconscious competence. This is when we don't really practice working with the mind, because it's become a natural part of our day; and we can find ourselves doing these things normally without a deliberate intent to engage in 'doing exercises'. For example, in situations that before may have lead us to anger, we may find a naturally greater resilience to what used to trigger us emotionally.

It's important to note that everything comes back to our attention and awareness, and as our understanding and experience of this develops more and more subtly, we will realise further benefits of this. The rest of the book builds on this idea, introducing more ideas and exercises to use a greater attention and heightened awareness for positive self and family outcomes. How we affect each other as members of the same family is worth more of our attention than we give, perhaps. For example, with a little awareness we can see how we elicit in others the very feelings we want to be rid of in ourselves (and theirs in us), whether deliberately or subconsciously so. Through this awareness, we can come to see that many of the conflicts and difficult reactions we have to each other within the family are caused by the feelings we project onto each other. This is often referred to as projective identification[9]. By working with our minds, we can expand our awareness of situations where we are 'wound up' by someone else, seeing what this entails from other perspectives than merely our own. By stepping outside of oneself in this way, we can consider how the person winding us up is feeling about the same situation. We can better question what may be winding *them* up, causing them to want to rid themselves of this feeling or pent-up emotion (whatever it may be) by foisting it onto others. The whole process of further reflecting on what we can do to help them deal with this challenge, and not to add to it or take on suffering of our own because of it, stems from being able to notice our own propensity to engage with the conflict and not the person. Seeing our own and others' states of mind more clearly is endlessly enlightening and helpful in this sense and getting the better of family interactions, challenging situations and our relationships with family members is helped by this enormously. We can explain, comfort, intervene, change environments, transform states of mind, encourage, and discipline ourselves and our family all the more openly, calmly and honestly through a greater awareness and by paying attention to each other.

Throughout the book we will refer to this process of working with the mind as a 'cycle', rather than as something that we complete. This is because even after reaching an unconscious competence we can observe an aspect of ourselves, our family or how life may change in respect to these, that perhaps takes us back to realising just how unaware we are again (this can be on a deeper level of awareness through prolonged practice). In other words, life is continually changing, and for us to take account of this in our individual and family endeavours takes focus over time, not just for a few weeks. Consider Aristotle's take on excellence – that it is not one day or a short time that makes us blessed and happy, that such virtue arises from doing the right actions over time. An 'excellent' family life then is hinged on being as 'excellent' as we can be ourselves. We're often in a constant subconscious search for self-comfort (as we'll explore in the coming chapters) and in this we find little truth, but as we consciously search for some self-truth we may find greater comfort. For some of us this may seem quite distant from our current experience, to deliberately pay attention to all the bits of ourselves that are challenging and negative. How is that we can accept this in ourselves without looking away, and how do we allow ourselves to pay attention to what's challenging or negative about ourselves and the conflicts we face? That's exactly what we'll discuss next.

Allowing and accepting

The world as we have created it is a process of our thinking.

It cannot be changed without changing our thinking.

*W*hy is it life is so hard at times?' In one form or another we invariably ask ourselves this question quite a lot and, however we frame this query, it highlights the fact that we don't care much for the difficult moments in life. Wouldn't it be great if we didn't have any of those?! Our reactions and emotions that arise because of life's difficult moments are so ingrained, they become the natural state of mind we experience in response to certain circumstances and situations. We sometimes don't even recognise any of the moments that gave rise to these feelings, but are still afflicted by them. So what can we do about this ill-feeling, the powerful negative emotions, and the challenging moments in everyday and family life? How do we rid ourselves of them? There's actually a simple solution to this, and by working with the mind we come to realise this through our own understanding and direct experience. It's quite profound really – the answer is *we don't*. We do not rid ourselves of negative, overpowering emotion, we don't look to remove ill-feeling from life, and we do not expect our life or family experience to be without challenge. These are elements of life that are important and natural, that we unhelpfully develop an adverse reaction to in some way. In this chapter we begin to lay the foundation for the positive change that comes through working with the mind. It comes down to willingness to change how we look at these parts of ourselves and our life experience. *Transforming* the negative is powerful and effective, trying to free ourselves of it is only destined to lead to further suffering.

It's normal to think, perhaps if only subconsciously, that we're pretty good at getting on with life as we are.

Engaging in the effort to change life as it is, and how we deal with it as we are now can seem an arduous and unnecessary task. However, it's actually only really through greater cognitive flexibility, or being more mentally adaptive, that we deal with changes in life with less resistance[1]. We tend to naturally find anything that pushes us outside of our normal operating state – even if only momentarily – quite unnerving. However, that normal state is often only 'normal' because it's become familiar and usual for us to think, speak and act in set ways; this is simply conditioned by a repetitive force of habit[2]. This doesn't actually make for a truthfully normal, healthy way of being. This is partly because there's no such thing anyway, but also because this just makes our individual habitual operating states of mind. Everyone's normal is normal! Merely recognising this and acknowledging that more can be appreciated by looking outside of our individual conditioned state, beyond our mere habit of being, we open up to potential that's greater than our normal operating state. This is also very true for how the family dynamic develops. We often never question whether it would be helpful to step outside of our comfort zone momentarily, regarding how we personally respond to and engage with family, and how we plan our lives and communicate our needs as a family unit. Something that's simply our particular state of familiarity, that's normal to us individually and, as a family, can collectively be thought of as our family's state of normal.

To allow ourselves to focus some attention on this status quo - and if there is any benefit to allowing an altered perspective on what's our normality – is interesting because 'if we do as we have always done, we get what we have always got'. This platitude sums up the current state of our most prevalent and influential states of mind quite nicely. If, for example we notice a persistent frustration in our dealings with loved ones, it may seem a tall order to expect this to change, and we see it as just a normal part of family life. They will, no doubt, still do what annoys us, we're obviously only human and will, of course, react to that – so how do we work with this to achieve more positive outcomes? If doing as we've always done gets us where we are right now, and we're looking for a better or more positive outcome, the realisation of a need to change our own approach to the frustrating situations we face is key.

To facilitate more love, support, happiness, or whatever positive outcome we seek from difficult family interactions, we have to put in more in terms of effort and enthusiasm to generate these in ourselves first. This effort and energy, a changing of where we allow our attention to roam and what we choose to focus on, is perfectly achievable. However in our habitual states of mind and comfort zone, our attention is directed automatically and subconsciously according to how we are conditioned as the individual we are. When in a state of comfort or familiarity with our routines, we are more often than not just functioning on autopilot (as we discussed in the first chapter). We act out similar responses to the same situations again and again. This results in more or less the same general outcomes, to the continued effect of reinforcing this reactive thinking, speaking and behaving. Continuing the example of frustration within the family setting, we can see this to be true because situations we find annoying don't tend to ever get less annoying by themselves! If we

43

take a new stance, perhaps consider why it's annoying to us, or think of it from another family member's perspective – only then, once we see our role in the annoying situation as integral to it being annoying, does it start to shift. This can be thought of as a process of allowing ourselves to explore challenging situations.

This 'allowing' is a powerful tool that lets us get out of our own way on occasion. This need only be for long enough to be able to let situations unfold, without trying to influence or react to them from a space of this normal operating state where we are normally inclined to pay attention only to the most annoying aspects. Quite miraculous and marvellous things can then occur, as we learn to facilitate and allow a shift from our current state of inherent, self-referential processing to take place (see **Figure 1.0** in the previous chapter).

'Allowing' is the process of being present and just *noticing* the current experience. From here, it is possible to draw back from the automatic perception of, or engagement with, the situation, event and circumstance as it arises and unfolds. We come to see outside the box by first allowing ourselves the awareness that our attention is solely focused within it. Allowing is best thought of as 'what we see when we look', whereas, usually, if we don't like what we see then we look elsewhere (and if we like what we see then we look with more enthusiasm and further expectation of enjoyment or entertainment). If what's there to see is neither exciting nor discomforting, the mind wanders a bit to see what else arises. In this manner, time is spent *doing* and not *being* for many of us, and this being present may perhaps seem like a strange notion to begin with. Think of this process as a practice for drawing back from oneself, or stepping out of oneself – as if you are a third-person observer. Allowing whatever's present to fundamentally simply be our current experience, is self-knowledge through not analysing or interpreting[3]. It involves awareness of how we're feeling, of what's going on around and within, thoughts, body sensations, speech and reactions, allowing the attention to rest wherever it stops, on whatever arises and comes to mind. Our awareness is not engaged with these objects of perception, but simply involves observing how we may be inclined to react to, then think about and want to do something in response to whatever is there. This state of mind becomes more familiar and accessible through the guided practices introduced in this book, where we include a deliberate anchor for us to return our attention to. So much happens as we allow ourselves to just *be*, that we are perpetually drawn back into the autopilot function and a subconscious mind awareness (where our attention is mostly automatically and subconsciously directed).

Just being is hard! The mind is keen to be active and forever attentive and we soon see our attention move to the next thing that arises, then the next, so rapidly at times we are not even consciously aware of it (without some practice to centre ourselves). Gradually, by subjecting the objects of our perception and experiences to a heightened state of awareness, which allows us to see, in turn, with less of an egocentric (or self-centred) concept of ourselves, we begin to start viewing whatever's going on in the moment as an experience *we* are having now, as opposed to how (or who) *we are* right now[4]. An important

45

distinction to make is that this allowing is not a process of removing oneself from difficulty, or avoiding situations and challenges. Allowing whatever is present to just *be*, whether neutral, positive or negative, isn't a lesser version of ourselves – in fact we actually become more capable in many ways. We are more free than our normal state of mind which is largely preoccupied with seeing how the self is affected: analysing, and judging outcomes and effects. *Allowing* is a sense of being with, adapting to, and observing whatever is present, without becoming engaged and entangled in it, or subconsciously caught up in thinking, talking about or reacting to it. Beyond this, allowing can be thought of almost as an intuitive sense of things. So when some difficulty does arise in our current experience, for example, we have a heightened sense of the experience rather than the cognitive processing, or thinking on and understanding of the experience and how we feel about it. Naturally, this all arises from some familiarity with the exercises involved. The specific implications for this on family life depend upon our particular family dynamic – but nonetheless the means by which we begin to benefit from this process, both individually and as a family, is the same. When faced with difficulty or challenge, if we have some grasp of working with the mind, our outlook is altered such that we are not as immediately and deeply drawn into the usual reaction we would be inclined to have in response to such a challenge.

In essence, our brains are shifted out of 'thinking' mode into 'experiencing' mode – from cognitive to experiential processing, which are theorised as two key mechanisms of how the brain processes information.[5] In the first 'mode', thinking about what happens, playing over situations and events in the mind, we see mostly how they have affected us and how it feels, which easily leads into further thinking about and possibly deciding what we wish to do about it in response. Thinking gives birth naturally to intention or desire to react, or to emotions, opinions and conversations about what happened. In many practices and traditions that guide us to greater awareness and resilience, a focus on the body is used to help us 'stay present'. More on this in the next chapter but, essentially, this helps us not to *rid* ourselves of thoughts and emotions but to observe the process of rumination, thinking and subsequent intentions and reactions that arise. So this second 'mode' is just of experiencing, which may seem as if we're not really doing much except noticing sensations in the moment. There is very little reaction to or thinking about it in the mind, it is just simply being with the experience at the time. Either mode of processing can be predominantly conscious, or subconscious, and with practice we can be more aware of this and deliberately choose to be cognitively or experientially responsive (or a balance of the two). The story below is of a brief experience I had in my early twenties, which illustrates an example of these two modes of processing information in the mind. With regard to any family situation that's difficult (with challenging thoughts, feelings, emotions, memories, situations and past events attached to it strongly), experiencing it directly rather than over-processing it cognitively offers an interesting approach. This requires us to have a few other skills in place if we are going to be able to separate the notions of how we think and feel about something, how it affects us and how we may react to it. We can then come to have an

awareness of the whole experience, instead of our attention being subconsciously carried away, or caught up and
automatically engaged in being lost in feeling, thought or
actions arising as a result.

It was early Sunday morning and I was slowly walking the quiet, empty streets whilst waiting for the
train station to open so I could catch the first train
of the day. Just idling away the time, I was aware
of the buildings, shops and paths in the stillness,
in contrast to the usual hustle and bustle. Looking
back I'd say I was quite present and mindful, just
paying attention to the walk and coming back to
this focus when my mind wandered a little.

I was walking out of town, on the path next to the
road leading into the city, and became aware that
over on the other side of the street a car was slowing on the road out of town. I didn't give it any further thought, because I was naturally engaged in
the walk and my own mind. Some shouts from the
car caught my attention again, which I remember
as "Oi! Fuckin' smack-head, I'll batter you out, you
cunt!" But I continued my walk that I was rather
enjoying; there were some intricate patterns to the
brick-work of some of the walls I passed, and quite
naturally my mind centred on the walking experience and away from thoughts of the four men in
the car I was intuitively aware of. I've come to experience since then, that when focused intently on
something, the other thoughts or objects of awareness have a distant, or less prevalent feel because
the mind is centred on something else. I somehow
had awareness there were four men, and that they
were probably clinging to the remains of some high

spirits carried over from Saturday night. I remember there being some notion somewhere in my mind of understanding that in another time on another occasion I could easily have been in the car, in not too dissimilar circumstances, on the opposite side of this experience. But this was all pushed to the back of the mind, awareness of the car stopping and someone crossing the road seemed intuitively less important than noticing the bus-stop I was approaching.

As the realisation entered my awareness that one of them was following behind me, the thought or perhaps intention came to 'just carry on'; it naturally seemed my attention was best placed on carrying on past the bus stop. Not much farther than the bus stop the assault happened. I wasn't really aware how close he was, but noticed the force of the blow at the back of my head trickle through the jaw and ear on the left side of my face, like concentrated pins and needles rapidly spreading, then everything turning white in my vision as I stumbled forwards. Then my vision returned, I regained my feet and the assailant disappeared back across the road to the car, almost becoming entangled with a cyclist whose path he violated on the way.

It was a strange experience, and I thought about it on the remainder of the walk before heading back to the station for my train. Anger and shame arose after the event when I began to reflect on how it felt, how I could have or should have acted differently. During the whole thing I never felt fearful or unsure, upset or angry or lost in thought and reacting, but just had the distant awareness in mind of the process unfolding as I was consciously and deliberately paying attention to my rather lovely walk. Once I had begun reflecting on it, my mind was firmly back in cognitive processing mode, and floods of opinions and emotions about the situation bubbled to the surface.

The story is interesting because it shows how we cause our own struggles much of the time, out of a difficult situation, making things in the mind much worse than they are. In this case, aside from an aching jaw for a few days, there were no lasting consequences, but the onslaught after the event such as a mind bent on revenge, guilt, self-doubt, shame, anger and resentment could easily have prolonged consequences beyond that of the event itself. Thankfully, this situation intuitively led itself to a balanced outcome, that I've no doubt would likely have been different if I wasn't in such an experiential mode during the event. I could easily have made a silly situation far more severe had the opinions and emotions been present during rather than after.

Allowing our attention to remain more fixed as opposed to naturally moving off, as it's inclined to do where something is difficult or uncomfortable, isn't always easy because we have an inherent drive to avoid any kind of discomfort. Indulging in activities that give us quick satisfaction, pleasure or gratification even extends to the habitual, subconscious mind. Really, our minds will do almost anything to avoid a fixed attention, and we see this as we notice the mind idly wandering, randomly thinking, and getting bored with routine tasks. Taming the unruly mind involves focusing attention on a particular thing, or set of things in our present-moment experience for an extended period. Add some difficulty or unpleasantness into this immediate experience, and the instinct or reaction to look away becomes especially strong. Look carefully a moment and think about it: who is it that truthfully benefits from such avoidance? Avoiding or disassociating with what's there, in essence allowing the autopilot, subconscious processing of what's going on, strengthens and further reinforces this cognitive habit of looking the other way. By overcoming this and giving everyday situations the required attention, (including the challenging ones) we learn, develop and grow ourselves instead of perpetuating this tendency toward avoidance. We need to escape saying and doing the same things, thinking in similar ways and enacting similar, reactive behaviour time after time, while still expecting things to go our own way, or for us not to have to experience challenges in life. We are so inclined towards this subconscious belief that we shouldn't feel bad when inevitable life challenges arise, that we have already disarmed ourselves. By already having looked the other way we are probably already engaged in making the situation far more significant, and more overwhelming than it actually is. To move away from being unconsciously so competent at disassociating when life doesn't go our way, towards being more competent at paying attention to a challenge and the learning opportunity it represents, we are better served through awareness, attention, allowing and accepting!

Over time these deeply-rooted negative or limiting frames of mind become the norm and we see that they are awkward to overcome. This is because what builds and accumulates is brought about by this subconscious expectation to be free from difficulty and suffering, we avoid being with this openly and just observing it, perhaps learning from it instead of reacting to it and repeating the same patterns of thinking, speaking and acting. Through working with the mind, we will see how becoming aware of our emotions and feelings[6] – including discomfort or suffering, and exploring reasons behind it – can help us take on different perspectives on challenges in our family life with progressive ease. When we're equipped to use awareness of our attention in such circumstances, we see when we are poised to react in ways that won't have a positive impact on the family or ourselves. We can allow ourselves to be as we are – learning from this observation as opposed to just being on autopilot with no awareness. Some common examples of this are shown in **Figure 2.0** below, that demonstrate how to avoid a situation in which we find ourselves on the other side of negative or destructive behaviour, speaking and thinking after the event.

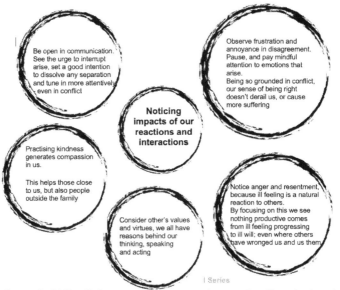

Figure 2.0 Mindful connections to enhance family relationships

Through working with the mind, we gradually recognise the precursors and links in the chain that lead to a conflict or challenging situations as such events unfold, or even before, by noticing in ourselves the subtle interplay that initiates the whole sequence of sensations and emotions involved[7]. A practical example of this can be thought of as the perspective change we can begin to implement in situations of conflict and frustration, where we have no control over something a family member does that frustrates us. We resort naturally to the basest of our emotions and responses in such circumstances, but allowing greater awareness of this and adopting a frame of mind that takes into account the point of view of the family member involved helps. We can see that our influence is a contributory factor, and that the perspective of others involved can also be taken into account. We don't have to like who we are or how we react, when this side of ourselves and these characteristics aren't as positive or beneficial as we'd like them to be. We all see ourselves differently from who and how we actually are, but our version of ourselves is the one we cling to as 'us'. Actually, if we see parts of us we don't like, this is a good thing; because we are *aware*, which is a powerful first step towards accepting ourselves as we are (and our experiences as they are).

Now, instead of ignoring this awareness, we need to allow this observation and accept what's present for what it is. We can then work with our efforts and attention to enable us to determine for ourselves that there can be some change for the positive. How we come across to other people, especially in the family unit, is far more of an indicator of what kind of a person we are than merely what we tell ourselves inside the private confines of our own head. When it comes to one's perspective of oneself (because this is only seen from our individual point of view), there is often no third person or outside perspective to say anything to the contrary, even though a third-person perspective of self is less biased. Working with the mind allows us to be like an outside person, observing ourselves and offering a different perspective – a greater acceptance – even if we don't have to like what we see immediately and, for some, looking truly at our own self is very difficult and painful. This is mostly because of what is in our past and present life experience, and more particularly, what kind of a person we see ourselves as being – in essence, who it is we tell ourselves we are in our inner thoughts and language. We do have to allow ourselves to be as we are, however, good, bad or ugly, and from this foundation of attention, awareness and allowing, we can begin to do something about accepting that we are as we are now. It is hugely freeing to accept that what happens to us in life is not perfect, but brings opportunity for self-growth, to come to grips with what troubles us, and what contributes to our limiting ways of interacting with ourselves and our loved ones. Wherever and whoever we are in life, we impact negatively on those around us at some point in some way, perhaps we shout at our family because of our own anger and frustration, hurt those dear to us, or set precedence within the family for poverty of ambition, low self-esteem and apathy. This needs to be observed openly and allowed before we can begin to accept our responsibility for ourselves, our actions and interactions with ourselves and within the family, and the effects that these have. Here, we truly have control and the ability to influence ourselves, rather than trying to change what happens to us, (although this is where our attention is so drastically drawn to) and on what we chose to do repetitively in reaction to what happens to us. This is also how we most effectively come to influence those around us, through the presence that naturally flows from our state of mindful awareness.

Ironically, although we very often can't do much about what happens to us, and inherently the mind doesn't like it when things are difficult or uncomfortable, discomfort is actually a good starting point from which to develop the skill of mindful acceptance[8]. It is something that we can become aware of frequently in daily life and when practising mindfulness exercises. Tension in the body and mind builds and settles quite naturally by itself, and thoughts and other reactions to this discomfort come quite instinctive, as no-one naturally enjoys being uncomfortable or in pain.

Stillness is vast and unnerving – try it for a few minutes and see what you can notice in the body and in the mind – this space will fill itself, and we see our natural inclination to never simply be as we are in the moment; even in the mind we are always 'doing, doing, doing'! As we'll see when we come to try some practice later (if we haven't before), we make a note of our sensations of discomfort as we're aware of them, and see how habitually the process of avoiding even slightly unpleasant sensations is hard-wired into us. We tend not to accept anything in life if it makes us feel ill at ease, and it's important to think about why. Everything we've ever learned comes first as the unfamiliar and uncomfortable, but somewhere along the way in life we begin to look at these new things as just unfamiliar and uncomfortable and unfortunately not as opportunities to learn.

Now, it's important to make it clear that working with the mind isn't about self-harm in any way, but allowing self-reflection and observation whilst ill at ease is a remarkable process. Where discomfort is slight, we can note it with friendly curiosity, observing ourselves realise the pain or sensation is unpleasant, and perhaps any other reaction to it we may experience in the mind. Attention can be returned back to an anchor again and again. Then, at times, the discomfort will ease on its own. We observe and understand the desire to act upon that awareness of discomfort, and subsequent chain of thought as to how we'll alleviate and avoid our suffering, and yet observe it a while longer. Then we see what happens to the discomfort, awareness of it, thoughts arising about it, and desires to be free from the discomfort. Then, as we re-adjust ourselves to relieve the growing tension in our mind or body, we do so with awareness, and deliberately, slowly - not as some automatic knee-jerk reaction to a desire we were barely aware of. This may seem a long shot from dealing with significant life changes, such as when hoping for, maintaining or developing a healthy, happy family gets really difficult. The process, however, is the same: we strengthen the habit of looking first, even where we seemingly need to act, and take account of what we can notice in our habitual state of reactionary awareness to what's going on.

Ultimately, self-control requires some level of this

self-awareness, and although this may all come across as hugely complex, with a little observance of simple exercises there's a continued growth in our ability to do this. It's not really all that complicated, and is more about maintenance of mind than alteration of mind. Fortunately, maintaining our minds need not add any burden to the flow of our day, and can, in fact, have an opposite, therapeutic and quite easing effect[9]. It's likely that as we set out learning about practising working with the mind, the intention may be to help establish a calmer, less stressed, less depressed, more emotionally capable and balanced frame of mind, outlook and perspective in life – in whatever guise may be most applicable to us and our situation. Consider for a moment the effect this may have on the challenge of family life, because it's important to understand that no amount of working with the mind will rid life of all challenges, conflict or confrontation! The same holds true for family life, in that working with the mind (and any other process, product, practice or philosophy actually) cannot remove the difficult, challenging and confrontational aspects of life within our particular family unit. As our individual self, and whatever our current family experience, there is always some level of self-difficulty, challenge and confrontation involved. So, we do not rid ourselves of negativity to try and cure life so that our experience is always positive[10]. We simply transform the current state of mind to allow us to accept experiences and engage in a more positive outlook on whatever situation we find ourselves in.

Often, the first thing noticed when beginning to practice fairly regularly or routinely, is that just taking some time out to step aside from the mania of balancing all our duties, responsibilities, tasks and worries can be immensely healing and beneficial. Practice is a loose term in working with the mind fortunately, and need only mean short periods of simple exercises as best fits our lifestyles and routines. The process of coming to allow, and to just 'be with' and accept what is, is integral to any and all of the outcomes of working with the mind towards improved family health and well-being, indeed, any outcomes beyond a focus on ourselves or our family as well. We need not set out to have greater awareness, attention, allowing or acceptance, but these are natural by-products of the mental focus and awareness exercises we engage in. The brain changes and psychological developments that naturally arise[11] mean we become progressively more able to interrupt this 'autopilot' state of life. We can often 'catch' ourselves during negative habitual responses, whether internally, whilst noticing how we think, or externally, in reaction to what goes on in life.

We will touch on 'how we want things to be', or our dreams, plans and goals for ourselves and family at various points in this book. This is partly because it's sometimes quite common not to have a clear idea of how we really want things to be – which we'll come to later in Chapter 8 – but also because it's important to realise the difference between how we want things to be, and how they are. This may perhaps sound obvious but, actually, we tend to see things (including how we want things to be) as how *we* are, rather than as how *they* are. For example, if we're feeling down and going through tough times, things that may before have been comforting, amusing, helpful and pleasant, may now be viewed as empty, annoying, a hindrance and distasteful. In other words, the same things, situations, circumstances and events have different effects and outcomes based on individuality and perspective[12], which changes greatly over time. If we see a frosty woodland scene with a presently pretty depressed frame of mind, and at a different time in life with a frame of mind of up-beat enthusiasm, the same sight may imbue very different thoughts, feelings, memories and associations in the mind. Without getting too wrapped up in this for now, perhaps just be aware that there are numerous times we are often caught-up in this continued (often subconscious) mental space. We think about how we want and expect things to be a certain way, but without any awareness of whether we (and how we think, act and what we focus on) are congruent to this desire. Especially when this is a powerful, emotional need (like more money, and resources to have a happy, healthy family life), we are easily drawn to the positive reality of this desire. It's easy to forget in this natural frame of mind the perhaps slightly less-pleasing reality of how things actually are (like not being as happy, healthy, wealthy etc. as we'd like). With this in mind, the process of practising so that we move towards acceptance becomes increasingly more important to consider; so that we can bridge gaps in our current family and life experience and what we'd like more of.

It is easy to mentally project what we want and how we see things, and this frame of mind influences how we go about getting them. These things we want and situations we plan for, aren't so right now because they are abstract. They are just nice ideas or thoughts of how we'd like things to be. For dreams to be real we must first give them attention and make them a goal, a little more solid than a dream, in that we want to achieve (or at least work towards) our goals. Manifesting the desire to work towards any kind of change or success takes motivation, then perseverance and, at some point, accepting that we don't have, but perhaps do not need, all the answers right now. If we knew what we had to do to get from A to B, but not from B to C or beyond then we are stuck. Similarly, if we know how to get from B to C, but not A to B; we're stuck. The process of building greater resilience through working with the mind doesn't require us to know how to take all the steps involved to get to where we want to be, just to notice if and when our actions and beliefs are limiting this progression. We soon see how this understanding and experience is of benefit to us. Then adapting the process of working with the mind to suit us and our routines is easy. Desired outcomes for ourselves and our family's journey can be realised more simply.

This is an important point to mention here, because life doesn't flow nicely from A to B to C to D and continue without any hiccups. Having some useful skills for being able to deal with whatever life throws at us is very helpful, especially when we find ourselves not knowing where we are in the flow of things, or how to get to where we might want to be. This is fundamental because, most of the time, most of our dreams or thoughts about how we'd like things to be stay just as they are – a dream or some nice thoughts[13]. With family in mind, if we leave these ideas or ambitions where they are, just somewhere in the space of the mind, what alternative is there and what outcomes do we see?

Without some form of planned direction, we risk allowing family to stagnate where it may flourish instead. This is not to suggest that merely by the wishing of it alone we can achieve the family or individual success we want, but to encourage reflection on the obvious fact that family is a collective, a group. However formed (there's no normal standard we can or should assign to family), this group functions by taking into account the needs and desires of those within it. And yet, how often is it that we honestly

- don't really establish awareness of, and acknowledge the collective needs and desires of the group or family unit?

- overlook these, preferring to just go through the motions of what lands at our feet?

- backtrack on any intention or effort towards these needs and desires, because it's too hard, or because we fear becoming stuck in the challenge involved?

- find our efforts and energies thwarted by other influences?

The above happens probably more often than we take time together, to be clear on our individual and group perspective on what our family stands for, and what it is we actually want for each other and ourselves. We can't accept our current state if we don't allow ourselves to pay attention and achieve an awareness of it, in which case it's useful to notice that it's easier and more natural to succumb to an autopilot state than to interrupt it. The limitation of this for family and the individual self, is that we choose to subconsciously disengage our minds from a greater awareness. The altered perspective of working with the mind, that we choose to instil consciously, engages our mind's awareness with noticing and accepting more naturally how we can go about improving our outlook on current outcomes, states of mind, ourselves and our family. Accepting is important because it enables us to remain in – and develop our control over – what we can immediately influence in life[14]. It helps us to let go of the negative impact of trying to control what's outside our sphere of influence, and enables us to see the difference between the things we can and cannot control[15]. The key is our input of effort and energy, and the focus we can bring to our worthy ideals, whether being better able to deal with the challenges of family life, or being more willing to work towards more positive outcomes for us and those around us – working with the mind helps us develop personal strategies to do so.

If talking in terms of manifesting our dreams into something real sounds slightly 'new-age', this is just the process of any creation. Consider the book you're holding for a moment – books need writing, paper, and printing. All these started as worthy or useful ideals – someone thought about them when they didn't exist. The idea of documenting and recording on clay tablets is thousands of years old, and using papyrus reed, bone, shell, wood and silk all came before paper was invented and adopted across different nations. So, this book you are reading is built upon a process of development, using the ideas and concerted efforts of people over thousands of years. Taking any other example really, the same process is true. All that we have and see was once an idea in the mind(s) of some individual(s) before it was worked towards and grad-ually realised as a change over time. By the same process, the more 'effort' we put into ourselves and our families, the more they and we gradually change, grow and develop. Working with the mind enables us to progressively see more clearly that our acceptable, common family-life values come from our own concept of family conditioned in us. This then presents another cognitive hurdle to be aware of – to come to allow and accept where our con-ditioning differs between family members. It may seem normal accepted behaviour to shout through the house for the attention of others within the family for some, and be normal to completely ignore others unless they come and talk to us face to face for other members of the same family! Interestingly, both behaviours may stem from the same value or need – that of wanting or needing to com-municate with our family and household. Although this is a simplified example of differences in opinion, feelings and behaviour, these differences are frequently a common source of frustration within the family[16]. Nevertheless they are easily reconcilable if those involved are all willing and able to have some awareness of each other's perspec-tive[17]. In effect, actually facing our difficulties together is the reason we develop together, and ignoring them from even one individual's perspective within the group can be a cause of us growing apart.

Such family development is best thought of as a pro-gression rather than as an end result; a journey rather than a destination, and the benefits we notice along the way help us in any overall change for the better. The importance of this is often culturally undervalued, as any process of self-development involves some level of arriving at concepts that help us in that moment which may have to be left behind later so that some new realisation and development can be achieved. Modern life allows us many areas to focus our efforts and energies, regardless of whether this is a good, bad or neutral thing for us, and it often leaves us and our families overlooked[18]. Taking time for oneself seems to come after work, duties, pressures, stresses and worries of everything that's vying for our attention today. This isn't even accounting for life's many entertaining and powerful distractions and intoxicants which can easily eat up all the energy and attention we have to give! It can seem that if something doesn't entertain us easily, happen quickly or keep us engaged without us having to exert any wilful effort, then it's not worth investing energy in. Fortunately, working with the mind need not take more than a few minutes of our time to begin with, and very quickly we may come to get more out of the time we do have by implementing some of these strategies and tools into our daily lives. Even where this means attention on the painful, the benefits and strength of this lies more in opening us up to accepting and dealing with the inevitable difficulty of family life; and not in feeling sorry for our lot in life.

What we get from working with the mind depends largely on the habitual frames of mind we have as individuals. If we are frequently or easily angered and stressed for example, and find ourselves forever short with those around us, such practices can support us to develop practical strategies for noticing what triggers this in us and what our habitual reactions to these situations are[19]. This then enables the process of seeing what influence and impact this has on our loved ones and relationships, of how we affect others and impart this way of being onto those nearest us (especially from a parenting perspective when a child's early stage references come from us directly). Very young children are especially adept at observing how we do things, and seeking some positive development in how our family dynamics unfold always begins with self-awareness, knowing more clearly how and why we think, speak and act the way we do in response to family situations. This is worth a small investment of effort, and if this naturally starts to accumulate with surprisingly little energy needed, then we can allow this process to unfold. More on the stages of working with the mind later, but it is worth mentioning now that we don't have to immediately love all the exercises and practices involved! They're just tools to introduce and guide our own understanding and experience, which is personal and that we will adapt naturally to suit our needs. So if some of the exercises introduced don't sit well with us, we need not despair. There are many ways of establishing more mindful perspectives and, with the right guidance, finding the methods that work nicely for us doesn't take long at all.

After noticing where our attention is placed, establishing greater awareness and allowing whatever arises to be present, we then come to the process of accepting what's there. This can be thought of as opening up to whatever occurs and arises in life. For example, when doing some of the practices we'll cover in the next chapter and then build on later, we may become aware of discomfort. The body may even experience pain if we have underlying ailments, or are still and too rigid for too long. Once we have our attention focused, are aware of the attention and what it's anchored to, are being present and are allowing whatever is there to be our present experience, accepting is a way of knowing (or at least telling ourselves) that this is OK. The mind will work hard to not have these layers of attention, to move away from awareness of attention, from allowing one's self to be present, and certainly from accepting what's there. So when accepting we don't turn away from or towards something – whether good, bad or indifferent – in our noticing of what's there, it is what it is. We accept it for what it is and not what we notice about it or how we react to or feel about it.

These are the first set of steps of the process of coming to work with the mind: attention, awareness, allowing, and accepting. It's important to remember this is a process, and we shouldn't expect to be overwhelmed with positive feeling the moment we begin practising some of the exercises. Every individual and family is different – and it's useful to bear in mind that each of us need to come to our own understanding and experience of ourselves and how we engage with our family unit around us. The working with the mind programme will guide us through this process towards a greater self-awareness. Then, from here, we can see that our attention is limited, that it can be used more wisely, and brought back to task once we're aware our mind has slipped into the comfy habits of dis-associating. This thinking literally changes the landscape of our life, as succinctly put by Einstein when he said we need to change our own thoughts if we wish to change our world. So notice the negative experience, reactions, states of mind and emotions in life, and realise the desire to be free of them. This is the opportunity to practice and strengthen our awareness, attention, and our ability to allow and accept. On to some exercises now to begin the practical part of this process.

Getting some practice started

As we're forever drawn into an object awareness greater than our awareness of self, we continually mistake what goes on in life for life itself.

We consider that which we experience to be our actual, individual self, rather than something that simply happens in our life at that point.

*I*n this chapter we start with some mindfulness-based exercises, and as with all endeavours in life, our frame of mind whilst doing this is important. At this point it may be outside our skill-set to be able to take account of our state of mind, and for now we'll concentrate on introducing the practices. Later the focus will shift on to what we may wish to hold in mind whilst engaging with working with the mind, and noticing our frames of mind and emotional state, as this leads nicely into some further practices. But, for now, a few things to consider to start with.

Prior to launching into any practical exercises for working with the mind it's important to manage our expectations, because looking at ourselves openly and how we are as an individual in life and within our own family can be quite tricky initially. What if we notice things about ourselves and how we speak, think and act around our nearest and dearest that we don't like? And what to do if we notice things about them that we don't like, that make us feel uncomfortable or bad? Perhaps whilst noticing the breath, a common anchor for mindful awareness practice that we'll come to shortly, we observe an increase in feelings of anxiety. Maybe whilst observing the body, another common anchor, we might intensify our awareness of pain, discomfort or trauma. Watching the mind includes deliberate awareness of thoughts and feelings, and this can be stressful when we don't like what we see. Where the idea of doing this seems abnormal, and when what we do see is initially quite difficult, this challenges us.

We'll progressively go into a little more depth on the idea of difficulty during the book, but it's important to note now that where our immediate experience of family life and our own individuality is especially hard, traumatic or involves deep suffering, watching the mind will likely involve awareness of difficulty from the outset. Fortunately for us, there is neither the necessity to understand, have prior experience of, nor even to enjoy these practices. The benefit of them is in the doing – even if what we notice at the time is particularly difficult. Our mind houses everything that's happened since birth, such as memories of the past, thoughts on the now and projections of what's likely to come based on our current life experience and understanding. Mind is very easily 'lost' in attention spent on thinking about the past or the future[1], and if much of this has been truly challenging, the mind's contents that we become aware of under scrutiny will likely be challenging to us at some point too. These are normal experiences that allowing for, accepting and not avoiding can be complicated or uncomfortable to do, as we begin our journey into using mindful awareness to work with the mind.

The exercise chapters of this book are progressive so that the practices are introduced sequentially. Each relies on some familiarity and comfort with the previous exercises. The first few introduced here are key, and these will form the basis of being able to get the better of the practices to come in Chapters 6 and 9. With this in mind run through each practice in order as they are introduced, using the guided audios available to support the exercise (more information on these soon). Then at the end of the book, refer to **Appendix 1) Further support** that will outline a programme you can follow to hone the experience and understanding of working with the mind through these exercises.

The length of practice varies according to comfort and need, and how our frame of mind approaching practice varies (see Chapter 8). It's quite common not to be able to sit in concentrated focus for some time, so as we notice any hindrance to following the audios and completing the exercises, know that with practice and more familiarity this is easier to settle into (we cover more about hindrances, or obstacles, in the next exercise chapter). 'Enquiry' after each practice allows us time to reflect upon anything we found difficult or challenging about each practice, and actually anything that arises from directing our attention inside of the space of awareness of the practice. This constitutes an invitation to reflect on anything in particular that was noticed during the exercise, and the process of enquiry is covered in the guided audios available, so make sure to refer to this prior to the practices. For now, this chapter will introduce some simple concepts and basic exercises to try, then we will build on these later. If at any point there are struggles with these, or overwhelming sensations that are difficult to deal with, the working with the mind community group is available to reach out to. There will be regular reviews of the community page on Facebook, if you need to reach out to the author or others with queries, or for guidance and support.

It will be useful to bear this idea of enquiry in mind when starting some of the practical aspects of working with the mind, because we're inclined to reflect only on what seems significant at the time. Whilst mindfully observing it doesn't particularly matter what is observed, so we are, in effect, reflecting briefly whilst enquiring after a practice period on what thoughts, feelings, intentions and anything at all that we were aware of. If it helps, think of the enquiry as a warm down after the exercise, in much the same way as we carefully ease the body back to normal after physical exercise – this is also the case with the mind after the mental workout of awareness and attention exercises.

Mindfulness of self begins with mindfulness of body and of mind, before we move into mindfulness of projections of body and mind, or other objects of perception like events and circumstances going on in our immediate environment. Ultimately, we do these practices to have clearer awareness of all projections of our perception in life; throughout the day and not just during the practice itself[2]. These 'projections' are everything and anything we notice whilst being aware of body or mind, perhaps thoughts, memories, distractions, sensations, feelings, impulses – anything. Finally we have mindfulness of self through heightened awareness of our interactions, and of everything that arises as we react and respond to our environments and situations. We have awareness of our thoughts, speech and actions in all situations whilst in a mindful frame of mind.

This may sound complicated, and as with all things, working with the mind is better understood via experience for ourselves. There is no theoretical understanding, or mere cognitive knowledge of working with the mind that is sufficient in and of itself alone. This must be balanced with experiential learning, through practice and doing and via direct experience. There is a personal balance to strike in this regard, and it's important to remember this is a process of learning that is unique to each of us. When starting out, and even after some experience, do not hold too many expectations, either of exactly how the process will unfold, or of any 'achievements' because of it – these will likely only become a hindrance to practice sooner or later. We may notice ourselves seeking specific outcomes, wanting to feel a certain way, to relive something pleasant that may have arisen before, or to avoid something we didn't like rather than just looking openly at whatever is. We will look at common hindrances to developing a mindful self-awareness whilst working with the mind later on in Chapter 6.

Within a particular 'space' of awareness (essentially what we're aware of right now), focusing on where attention is placed determines whether consciousness is centred internally, or engaged in focus on the objects of consciousness. This isn't a crude separation to mean body and mind or what's inside and outside, but rather to point towards what it is that does the observing, with attention on the observing itself not on the object of observation. If this perhaps still sounds a little esoteric, we will begin with a few simple exercises to cover the process of anchoring our attention and strengthening our awareness 'muscle'. Anchoring simply means having a chosen point or object to focus our attention on to[3] – and this can be any object, sensation, thought or memory – actually anything we can use as a point of focus to attach our attention to. With familiarity we will come to a point of having greater awareness of which particular anchors work well for us under different circumstances, and we may come to use and switch our attention between many anchors. As we develop the skill of using our focus of these anchors, we come to observe ourselves in an interesting fashion. Where our mind is occupied in the task of paying attention and establishing awareness, we see what else arises without needing to react to it or to engage with it. This is a very subtle change in perception, again one that is better understood through personal experience as well as understanding. We just watch things pass through our awareness, and continue with our practice of focused attention, maintaining awareness of this attention and where it moves.

The anchors we'll start with are the breath and the body, because they're free to use and always present, but also because they form the foundations of further practices for establishing a mindful awareness. Breathing mindfully, and a mindful awareness of the body, can make a more centred frame of mind immediately accessible with repetition and familiarity. In fact with surprisingly little practice we can return to a calmer, less reactive state from even the most influential and agitated states of mind[4]. Greater awareness of breath and body itself can be sufficient practice for us to undo much of the limiting and challenging frames of mind and experiences in life. In fact, the benefits of all the exercises to follow these quite naturally arise as a product of deepening and adding to the focus on breathing and body anchors.

Finding our own balance when making these useful to achieve our best possible outcomes is a personal journey. The only suggestion made here is that you run through all the exercises first to establish the use of the process as a whole. From here, adapting it to individual needs becomes more feasible. Much research and review of current liter-ature surrounding such practices suggests that 8 weeks' practice is the period where noticeable changes to the functioning of the brain occur akin to those in long-term practitioners[5]. Treat the exercises in this book as if fol-lowing a course, allowing sufficient practice with each before moving to the next. Also see **Appendix 4) Practice plan** for more ideas and support on structuring practice to suit individual needs. There is no substitute for experi-enced, accredited support from a qualified instructor, yet the next best thing which is as important to implement, is guided practice to try at home to supplement our learn-ing and development of our own practice. To this end two simple practices are detailed below to begin with.

Breathing Mindfully

When establishing an anchor for our attention on the breath (refer to **Figure 3.0**) there are three main locations where it is likely we can notice the breath most clearly. We breathe throughout the day and night usually unaware of the breath. When deliberately focusing our attention on the breath, we do not need to think about taking breaths in or out, just to notice that the breath comes and goes and observe the sensations involved. This underlies a key principle of practising mindfulness: we are not identify-ing with things that arise in any space of awareness, we are just experiencing them as they are – observing them clearly[6]. The sensation of noticing the breath is likely to be experienced as a passage of air, movement of mus-cles, pressure, a flow of air round the mouth and/or nose, whichever is most prevalent or a mixture of all of the above.

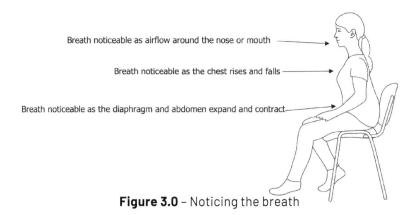

Breath noticeable as airflow around the nose or mouth

Breath noticeable as the chest rises and falls

Breath noticeable as the diaphragm and abdomen expand and contract

Figure 3.0 – Noticing the breath

Steps to follow during the **Breathing Mindfully** exercise are laid out below, but remember to make use of the guided audios that are available. Take about a minute to 90 seconds for each of the steps below, until you feel more comfortable and familiar with them to extend this gradually and without the audio. Perhaps read through the steps first, to gain an understanding of what the practice involves, then follow the guided audio practice without the book. First find somewhere to sit, upright if possible and where you can be uninterrupted for a few minutes.

- Settling into a comfortable seated position on a chair or the floor as preferred, take a few series of breaths in and out to establish where the breath is most easily noticed. If it helps perhaps lengthening the cycle of the breath, so that in breathing more deeply than normal it may become easier to notice the movements and sensations involved.

- Perhaps hold a hand lightly over the chest or abdomen, to gain an awareness of the rise and fall with the in and out breath.

- Keeping an upright but not tense posture, holding the back straight with the chin slightly tucked in. Making sure not to lean too far forwards or backwards, and keeping the shoulders back and relaxed in a natural posture opening the chest; but most importantly find a comfortable but alert balance without slouching.

- If it feels comfortable perhaps closing the eyes, or lowering the gaze whilst doing this; which should help focus the attention more completely.

- Notice the movements of the breath, gradually increasing the range of movement; so the cycle of the breath is longer – until breathing in and out as fully as possible to our own level of comfort. Really tuning the attention in to the movements of the breath in the abdomen or chest.

- This time slowing the movements down, taking as long as it feels comfortable to complete a few cycles of the breath in and out. Where the mind wanders off, and notices thoughts, sounds, other things, then gently guiding the mind back to paying attention to the breath.

- For the next few breaths allowing the cycle to shorten, gradually decreasing the range of movement; shorter and shorter until breathing in and out as light and shallow as it feels comfortable to do. Each time the mind notices anything else, just reconnecting to this anchor of the breath, and the short, light movements.

- Allowing the breathing to return to a natural rhythm,

depth and pace; perhaps following the movements as they arise, and not controlling the breath in any way.

- In your own time, bringing the practice to a close, taking a few moments to allow any lingering awareness of the practice to subside.

- When it feels comfortable, raising the gaze or opening the eyes

This exercise strengthens awareness of the breath in the body as a tool for using our attention more completely. It may feel strange at first because the forces of distraction are difficult to resist[7] and the mind is accustomed to a wandering focus, and yet here we are observing ourselves with a fixed attention on the breath as it cycles and repeats. We are not concerned about how the mind moves our attention, or how it is distracted and how this may make us feel, nor the wider contents of the mind particularly. This is because *we're just watching the movement and sensations involved as the breath comes and goes*. In the **Breathing Mindfully** exercise we are becoming more deeply aware of the breath, paying closer attention to the in and out movements, and keeping our attention there for a short while. Just observing and being aware when our attention moves away from the breath to anything else, then when we're aware some attention has moved from the breath we observe this. This is natural and such distraction may happen many, many times during practice. We use this awareness of our attention to focus the mind back onto the anchor of the breath, maintaining that awareness that we are consciously anchoring to the breath each time we notice the attention has moved elsewhere.

Appendix 4) Practice plan, details where to access a free practice plan to guide ongoing use of these exercises, and which also shows where to access in-depth, guided audios to support this. We will delve a little more in detail as to why these kinds of practices have the effect they do, how the brain develops, and, in Chapter 5, will also review the development and standards of modern mindfulness practice. Whatever our current level of understanding and experience, it's important to always work towards furthering the balance of it. Ultimately, working with the mind goes beyond single-pointed concentration in order to have the ability of making awareness itself that object of focus. Body and mind are the means, or the vehicle through which life is experienced, and we function by following the process of taking in information from the infinite and filtering it to the finite. This creates the journey we go through, one which we have really very little control over in the grand scheme of things. Having a growing understanding and experience of this process through a progressively greater awareness, helps us to pinpoint those aspects of self that hinder our individual self and family development and cohesion.

If it feels difficult, or initially unhelpful to include time for such awareness in our day, this is because it can seem much easier to simply go through the day in the usual automatic manner. Changing habits won't come without some resistance, and the mind can be quite persistent in being resistant! Despite this reluctance to change which is natural and should be expected, allowing time for some settling of the awareness before, during or at the end of our day is never truly a hindrance to daily life. It may seem this way because we are inclined towards allowing our attention to automatically wander. Nevertheless, going through the process of reigning in an unruly mind to a focused attention is helpful on many levels. It allows this process of greater acceptance of whatever is there, be it good, bad, beautiful or ugly and whatever's in-between. Chapter 8 discusses the importance of using aspiration, inspiration and motivation guided by our growing self-awareness, to counter the mind's inherent desire to recoil back to a seemingly blissful, inattentive and disassociated state of autopilot (along with the more destructive frames of mind and habits that go along with it).

Body Scan

A heightened sense of mindful awareness of the body has useful implications in day-to-day life. We all have various signals in the body that arise from things like pain, anxiety or stress signals and headaches. Increasing our ability to 'tune into' and be aware of our body's signals is a useful tool to become aware of what's going on within us, because most of the time we are unaware of how the body is feeling[8]. This in turn helps us to do something about alleviating building tension, stress and the frames of mind that contribute to or arise out of them. This heightened awareness of the body can also have interesting implications when we're in exaggerated, energetic or emotive states of mind as they arise frequently in everyday and family life. Have you ever tried, for example, to notice how the body feels during a really frustrated state? Try it next time you really get mad with a loved one or anyone else – quickly scan the body using this practice and see what you notice.

To begin with, this exercise will simply introduce the idea and experience of focusing attention around the body. In practical everyday terms, however, we can begin to see that the states of mind we're habitually inclined to reside in are actually reflected in the body as well. So some level of ability to tune into the body further enables us to notice when some difficulty arises, and to see the effects this can have on us and those around us through our reactions to it.

For this exercise, whilst maintaining awareness of the breath, we will introduce a 'scan' of the body. Here we move or 'scan' our attention from head to foot, to see what we can be aware of in the body. The **Body Scan** exercise involves paying attention to different parts of the body as a focus to anchor our attention to in a given moment. When we start focusing on the body the goal is to just be aware of any present sensations and feelings, not to react to them or to seek specific sensations or feelings. Interestingly, what is in the mind is also in the body, and the other way around. We shall see this more clearly after some experience using the **Body Scan** meditation.

With practice we may come to see the effects that stress and other psychological conditions have on us phys-iologically. This means that thought pattern and psycho-logical form affects our bodies, or the physiological form. The mind and body are not entirely separate, most simply because what affects one affects the other, but today it is more intricately understood than this. 'Bodymind', a term for understanding the body and mind as an indivisible unit, goes beyond 'mind over matter' thinking. Although we naturally assume the mind is of the body, actually the body is also of the mind, noticed by and experienced in the mind. Our entire representation of our physical self is the extension of the mind, and we can come to our own understanding and experience of this for ourselves. The scientific explanation for body and mind being one is becoming increasingly coherent. There is greater understanding of the brain networks that form very specific communication chains throughout the body, via neuropeptides and receptors understood to translate sensory information from body to brain and emotional state from brain to body[9]. Some studies have indicated that attention on purely the physical can cause a redistribution of perceived mind, strengthening the perception of emotion and sensation, whilst weakening the perception of action and self-control[10]. Using understanding and experience of the bodymind we can start to work back through situations that have challenged us, such as encounters, reactions, illnesses and periods of difficulty in life that we can recall from family confrontations or difficult situations we face. We can reflect on such occasions within our family unit to remember the process that unfolded, for example when we have reacted with impatience and frustration. It's possible to begin to remove much of the suffering from how we perceived the occurrence, to see more dispassionately how the process unfolded. It becomes easier after this to progressively observe this process unfolding, like connected links in a chain in real-time. The next time a similar chain of events occurs and we notice this impatience forming, we can use a more mindful frame of mind to switch our attention, perhaps even with reduced impact and less of a negative effect on us and on our loved ones. In fact, this is the process by which we can come to try and see from their perspective instead of ours, even when we may not agree with it.

It is important (at this stage especially), not to hold on to too many expectations from practising these exercises. In time and with experience and understanding, they will come to contribute towards significant effects on things such as noticing impatience, or even anxiety, anger, stress and depression that all impact upon our interactions within the family and how we affect each other. Actually, many areas where we may choose to consciously react and exert a different response rather than acting out the same habitual response patterns to the same detrimental effects, are all the better served through practising mindfulness-based exercises. Once we start looking at understanding our thoughts, emotions, frames of mind, sensations and discomfort, we will see more clearly that one affects the other, and that our body and mind are perhaps more interconnected than we realise. We can begin to notice earlier on in chains of events where we are triggered to a point of reacting detrimentally, or notice a situation that we have no influence to sway. This is most useful where we see the outcomes of situations as a negative, and can then at least cause no further harm to ourselves or others involved, and come away from it with reduced suffering.

The steps to follow during this exercise are laid out below, and as with the **Breathing Mindfully** exercise it's helpful to read through the steps first to gain an idea of the entire practice, then to do the exercise guided by the audios available. For this practice you can sit, stand or lie down but if you choose to lie down bring your heels and feet resting on the floor up to meet the bottom and lower spine, so that your knees point up with the legs bent and not lying flat. This will flatten the lower back and reduce any tension from building there. Feel free to use a pillow or cushion under the head too if this feels more comfortable.

- Perhaps sitting or lying down making yourself comfortable somewhere you'll be warm and undisturbed. Allowing the gaze to gently lower, or of it feels comfortable to do so closing the eyes

- Taking a few moments to get in touch with the movement of the breath, and the sensations in the body that are connected to the breath. Feeling the abdomen or chest rise as the breath comes in, and lower as the breath goes out.

- When ready bringing the awareness to physical sensations in the body, especially to any sensations of touch or pressure where the body makes contact with a chair, or the floor or bed. On each out-breath allowing ourself to let go of the focus on other things that we can be aware of.

- Settling a little deeper into awareness of just these physical sensations that are present. Reminding ourself of the intention of this practice, not aiming to feel any different or bring about a state of relaxation or comfort. This may happen or it may not, instead the intention of the practice is, as best we can, to bring our awareness to any sensations that we can detect as we focus attention on each part of the body in turn.

- Bringing awareness to the physical sensations and noting the patterns of sensations as the breath comes and goes. Taking a few moments now, feeling the sensations of breathing in and breathing out. Noticing how this feels in the body.

- Having connected with the sensations of the breath, now bringing the focus or spot light of awareness down the left leg and left foot, out into the toes of the left foot, focusing on each of the toes of the left foot in turn.

- Bringing a gentle curiosity to investigate the sensations that maybe there, perhaps noticing a sense of contact between the toes, a sense of tingling and warmth, or no particular sensations. When it feels comfortable, on an in breath feeling or imagining the breath entering the lungs, and then passing down through the abdomen, the left leg and foot, then out into the toes of the left foot.

- Then on the out-breath feeling or imagining the breath, coming all the way back up out of the toes and foot, through the leg, abdomen and chest and out of the lungs.

- As best we can continuing this focus for a few breaths; breathing down into the toes and back out from the toes of the left foot. If it is initially difficult to follow the breathing in this way, just noticing this, and as best we can approaching this observation openly, playfully, before focusing again on the flow of the breath.

- Breathing in and feeling or imagining the breath passing from the lungs, leg, foot and out into the toes of the left foot. Then on the out-breath feeling or imagining the breath coming all the way back up and out.

- When it feels comfortable letting go of the awareness of the toes, and shifting the awareness to the sensations on the bottom of the left foot. Bringing a gentle investigative awareness to the sole of the foot, the instep, the heel.

- Perhaps noticing where the heel or the sole of the foot make contact with the floor, or where the foot is resting. Experimenting again with breathing into the sensations present, being aware of the breath in the background, whilst exploring the sensations around the bottom of the foot.

- Allowing awareness to expand to the rest of the foot, to the ankle and top of the foot. Just noticing whatever sensations may or may not be present. Over a series of slightly deeper, prolonged breaths, directing the attention down into the whole of the left foot noticing whatever can be observed there.

- On the next breath in allowing the awareness to move into the lower left leg, around the back into the calf muscle, and the shin bone at the front. Slowly rising up the leg scanning with the awareness for any sensations that can be noticed.

- Matching the flow of the breath with the slow shifting of the focus up the left leg, into the knee, around the front of the kneecap, the back of the leg behind the fold of the knee. Continuing the gentle curiosity, this scanning of our awareness to any physical sensations in the upper left leg, where the thigh connects to the hips.

- In the same way, moving this attention out into the toes of the right foot, repeating this scan on the right side. Noticing the sensations present there before scanning the awareness, breath by breath, upwards from the bottom of the right foot all the way to the upper right leg. Just noting any sensations that you can be aware of, whilst breathing into those areas.

- Over a series of breaths, bringing awareness to the lower back, noticing any sensations and feelings within the body here. Following the breath, slowly scanning the awareness upwards into the upper back and across the shoulders, breathing into any sensations present.

- Now bringing the attention to the abdomen and stomach, perhaps noticing the movements here associated with each breath coming and going. Slowly moving this attention upwards into the rib-cage and shoulders, observing anything that is present. Gently scanning the armpits for anything that can be felt.

- On the next breath out, letting go of any awareness of this region of the body, and starting to move this awareness into the tips of the fingers of the left hand. Whilst breathing slowly, working up through the hand, arm, elbow, upper arm and back into the shoulder. Noticing what can be present there.

- Awareness in the mind will wonder away from the breath or the body from time to time, that's entirely normal during this practice. This is what minds do! When noticing this, just gently acknowledging where the mind has gone off to, before gently returing the attention to the last part of the body we were focusing on.

- Repeating this process on the right arm, starting with awareness of the tips of the fingers of the right hand. Working slowly upwards to the shoulder.

- Bringing awareness now to the neck, and the top of the spine at the back of the neck. Noticing, exploring, observing any sensation in and around the neck.

- Slowing scanning upwards in sync with the breath, noticing any sensations around the back of the head, the side, around the ears into the jaw and the face. Scanning the awareness for anything that can be noticed whilst coming up to the top of the head, and breathing into those sensations present.

- Having scanned the whole of the body, taking a few breaths to notice a sense of the body as whole, with the breath coming in, and out of the body.

- Gently releasing any focus from this practice, expanding the awareness to the surrounding environment. When it feels appropriate opening the eyes or raising the gaze.

Attention on the body needn't always be as in-depth as this practice, and in **Appendix 1) Further support** you can access some guided practices using the body-scan principles in a less prolonged and formal way. We'll come to 50:50 awareness, and practices for this soon. This **Body Scan** practice will help us develop awareness, firstly of ourselves in the immediate context of what's going on in the body, and what we can sense and feel there. As we repeat and progress further with the exercises in this book, we gain understanding and experience then gradually get more familiar with working with the mind.

Considering family, this enables us to be aware of the others around us, specifically to see that there are always many perspectives on the topic at hand. By starting with a greater awareness of oneself, we can then more easily proceed to being able to notice when and how we react to those around us within the family, and how they, equally, may be inclined to respond and react to situations. We see what situations we tend to gravitate towards dealing with more positively or productively than others, then also where we don't engage as well, and the implications of this for us and our loved ones. Repeat these exercises until they are comfortable and familiar, making sure to make use of the guided audio tracks that will support this. It won't be long before we quite naturally take on a greater awareness of life, beyond the time that we spend actively practising awareness and attention exercises. At this point we may come to think we know our established practice and the benefits it has. A word of caution at this point in light of this potential: it's easy to think about practice and become philosophical, but without doing the exercises as well there is little benefit. There must be a practical experience of using these techniques as regularly as befits our routines, because to know and not to do, is not to know[11].

We can even come to some awareness of the nature of the attention of other people, and can open up the opportunity for empathy and compassion through this – we will come to that later with more practices. We can use this awareness, and a mindful state of mind, to find a less destructive or more rounded response, appreciating that our immediate intended reactions to this may need initially observing before allowing to unfold. This is made possible where we have an awareness that enables us to notice how arriving straight at a place of frustration causes us to react negatively. How we tend to think, speak and act when this occurs may not illicit a productive (or even our desired) outcome. Reflecting on extreme examples of where our innate emotive reactions can lead may be useful for some of us, because the same process arising is present in all of us no matter how extreme the resultant outcome and behaviour. Although extreme cases have more unfortunate outcomes, which we'll touch upon a little later on in Chapter 7, it can help to include focus on this for some of the exercises to come.

Figure 3.1 – The ABC model of emotions

We often react to situations and feel emotions through

familiar and habitual ways, as the brain has very established categories for processing information and experiences. The ABC model of experience in the above **figure**,
shows A as the situation, B the interpretation and C the
outcomes from the situation occurring. It is easy to think
that the situations we experience in life have the most
sway over what happens to us and how we feel - using the
ABC model that A leads straight to C. The situation occurs
and this is what happens as a result of it, but when we
realise that our interpretation of events – what we think
and believe about them – holds most sway in how we are
affected by it, we find ourselves empowered to overcome
some of the difficulties of emotional states and ways of
reacting to challenges in life.

Before we move onto any other activities for working
with the mind, it's important to consider 50:50 awareness.
This becomes an increasingly important part of adapting
some of the more formal and purely mindfulness-based
practices involved in working with the mind into daily life
in a less formal way. In time, doing the practices introduced so far, those that we'll come to, or any other practices that some of us may already have some experience
of, we come to notice a heightened sense of awareness.
This is an experiential thing, and will be described differently by everyone.

Essentially it's the state of mind and body we can enter
as we begin to settle a little deeper into our awareness,
which can feel very slow and calm. Although this is nice it
is not always practical to assume we should feel this way
after every practice; nor should it be something that we
seek out. There has to be a practical and personal balance

struck with using these practices, as we and our family will not always be better served by us assuming a heightened sense of awareness on everything and anything that occurs in daily family life! This is where the idea of 50:50 awareness comes into its own. This is where we are aware of an anchor, but not to the point where our attention is placed solely on this anchor, and we are drawn into a heightened space of awareness and any ensuing pleasant stillness with it. Clearly, this isn't always practical in the hectic experience of family life! Bringing our attention back to an anchor again and again in an extended (longer) practice, can have quite profound results. However, short exercises are no less useful, and can be easier and more practical to implement during our busy lives. There are some free PDF downloads available as a bonus with this book, that support a 50:50 awareness and some more family-oriented practices: see **Appendix 1) Further support** for these and all other additional content. Whilst reading this part of the book, also take a moment to notice what your feet feel like. Perhaps they're resting on the floor. Is it cold? Is there a sensation or feeling of temperature or pressure and touch where the feet are resting? Just notice what the feet are doing, perhaps a foot is tapping or maybe there is stillness. Prior to this invitation to notice, what were the feet doing? It's likely that they were doing the same as after we began this brief investigation, but placing our attention deliberately on the feet momentarily allowed some awareness of this. Before our attention was just (mainly) on the reading. This is 50:50 awareness. We're still able to 'do' normal things, engage with the duties of the day and our usual interactions, but we also take a moment to establish brief awareness of an anchor for our attention – in other words, to centre ourselves. This deliberately grounds us in the present moment, and can make it easier to build a practice that we can adapt into our day rather than as a formal practice where we sit for some time deliberately away from the distractions of the day. This will become an important part of working with the mind from the family perspective, because it may not always be possible to take lots of time for formal, deeper practices. These are well supplemented with shorter or impromptu mindful moments of awareness which break the autopilot of the day. This is especially valuable in the build up to, during and after a conflict or confrontation, as we review anything we can be aware of with respect to how we reacted. We may have exacerbated the situation, or contributed to it in some negative way. We'll introduce a practice in Chapter 9 that further builds on this, so we can start to use these circumstances and events to see what thoughts, words and feelings we notice in ourselves in the moment and how these affect the situation or conflict arising.

So, fundamentally, 50:50 awareness can be extremely useful in our day-to-day practice, because modern life and family responsibilities can often make prolonged routine practice more challenging to fit in. Consider what use a regime of prolonged morning practice is, if in the period between this practice we are lost in autopilot, never noticing ourselves going through the day-to-day business of family life. We will develop on the importance of this when we come back to more practices later. For now, know that working with the mind will involve finding our own balance, finding what mix of these practices best suits our routines and needs. And don't worry! We will be going over exactly how to do this in the coming chapters so we can develop our own appropriate resilience to the mind continually processing what happens to us by reference to our own ego or sense of self. Wherever we are, whatever is going on and however we feel at any particular point is something we can use. No matter how challenging or difficult the contents of the mind there is always the option to be mindful of it – so whatever is in the mind, use it! Now we have some idea of working with the mind, we come to consider how to understand and experience where our practice may be of benefit to our family life, and how to focus on advancing our practice as we'll come to this in the next chapter.

Acknowledging and advancing

There are no facts, only interpretations

*I*t's all very well doing some personal mindfulness practice, thinking about self-awareness and where our own attention is placed during our habitual frames of mind, normal situations and events, but what of the family at large? The most important and influential person in our family (as you may have guessed) is oneself. It is ourselves that we can control, and it's our own reactions, intentions, thinking, speaking and acting that we can change for the better. Our family is only ever better served by us being the best version of ourselves we can. In this chapter we will look at the mind, and how our different states of mind influence the whole of the family. Whilst being aware of and then allowing and accepting what habits of self we have, we notice our tendency to react detrimentally to what arises each day and our impact on our family. A model for the mind can be useful to work from whilst considering this, and how we can use attention to more wholesomely refer to ourselves. **Figure 4.0** introduces a simple model for the mind that can be helpful when thinking about our states of consciousness.

Consciousness itself needn't be overcomplicated or even to be understood to benefit from this book, but it's important to note that our individual understanding of mind is arguably still not that developed in today's modern world. This contributes to the many challenges we're faced with today, despite our reasonable states of affluence and comfort relative to our needs. Our inability to pay attention to the mind and think outside of our common frames of reference only makes the negative more negative, and the positive less noticeable and appreciated in life. Everyone knows someone suffering some life-limiting health concern, whether physically, or through stress, anxiety, depression or simple inability to get the better of difficult and self-inhibiting states of mind. Yet few of us know anyone with experience, awareness and support enough to do something preventative and restorative about such concerns, and the more limiting and detrimental states of mind they have experienced. This self-awareness leans towards more holistic healthcare services, and individual approaches to health and well-being. Although easy to associate with being unscientific or 'hokey', in the healthcare sense, 'holistic' simply means thinking about health and well-being with regard to the whole person. This includes taking into account mental and social factors, rather than just the symptoms of a disease or cause of difficulty. Physical health seems the current conventional measure for our thoughts, services and outcomes on health[1].

For overall well-being, however, we are becoming gradually more accepting of advice and support for other dimensions of health. Conventional systems and services look to integrate mental and physical support. A good example of this is the IMPARTS Research and Education team. Their information sheet in **Appendix 6) Bibliography** shows some good examples of support from the health service to consider this body-mind link, and how to look at different ways to manage physical symptoms and emotional well-being[2].

In noticing aspects of ourselves that have negatively impacted on family, we shouldn't be looking to cure or fix the mind. These aspects of self that we notice as a hindrance to normal family life, are opportunities to establish a more positive means and method of working with the mind instead. The whole purpose of working with our own mind, realising and accounting for the contents of it, is to add to and enhance the important experiences in our lives[3] – family being one of the most crucial. Regardless if family experience is largely positive or negative, this process is invaluable!

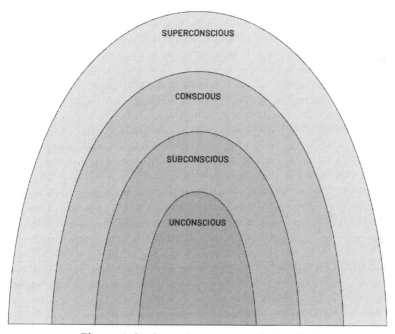

Figure 4.0 – Conscious states of the mind

Figure 4.0 represents the idea that the basic states of consciousness aren't unrelated, something that we intrinsically don't have much awareness of normally. We tend to feel that this moment is all there is, and our thoughts, feelings and state of mind in this moment is a stand-alone state, unaffected by our numerous other states of mind. If one state of mind influences another in some subtle way, then we can deliberately effect a change in how we subconsciously and habitually come to interact in the world, through working with how we deliberately and consciously do so. The seeds of how we do act, the roots of all our habitual speaking, thinking and behaviour are sown into the different conscious states of the mind, which also store everything that we don't have awareness of through conscious attention[4]. This means that we can deliberately focus our attention on the most prevalent tasks at hand as we go about the day. Our conditioned mind has learned from every second of life's experiences, and these seeds are forever dormant in the subtler states of consciousness; always able to take root under favourable conditions. Has a film, piece of music or conversation snippet from many years previous ever randomly popped into your mind, seemingly unrelated to what was going on at the time? This is quite common, as the contents of the mind can be quite random – which is a familiar experience for some when working with the mind. This also suggests why our habitual reactions and emotional responses to things are so immediate, because we normally have a diminished awareness of these subconsciously taking place until noticed in the conscious mind as direct experience. When working with the mind we progressively see these things as they unfold, not after they have formed, and consciously acknowledging what's in the mind becomes easier.

When we observe some deliberate quiet, often what arises in the mind is instinctively quite noisy to fill this space. This 'noise' can come from any of the stored memories and prior experiences we've ever had. Our attention and energy to concentrate (or 'executive function' as it is referred to scientifically) is finite[5], and if we consciously had to regulate all our attention, just imagine what we would have to be aware of moment by moment! Just sitting – even if we weren't reading this book and in the absence of tasks – the brain still shows structured changes in activity of the neurons[6]. Our five major senses are forever busily gathering information from inside the body and the world around us into the brain to be processed. Sight is light energy relayed to the brain as electrical impulses via the optic nerves. Sound is waves of energy and vibration sent to brain through the ears. Taste, touch, smell, internal signals from the digestive system, organs and various body parts are all signals interpreted by the brain so we can understand what's going on in the body and our world at any one point. This sensory input is just data interpreted by the brain, and may stimulate the growth of some seed of thought or prior similar experience and memory at any point. Acknowledging this is the next of our steps for working with the mind as there is often a significant lack of any real acknowledging that right now, life is how we currently interpret these signals, this data that we perceive from our immediate experience. This is something that, with practice, we can ultimately have greater control over, and the progressive realisation of this through increasing familiarity with the exercises involved is very profound. It ultimately enables this movement of practising awareness and attention exercises towards being able to use our focused mind for more positive outcomes within our family unit, as we'll explore over the next few chapters.

Practice in the context of the book is to help us know ourselves better, to acknowledge aspects of ourselves that limit family growth and development, and to help us develop strategies for allowing difficulty and confrontation. Within the modern family unit, this goes a long way in supporting us to establish a frame of mind from where we can more constructively respond in times of difficulty and heightened emotions. Looking from outside of the perspective of self alone and accounting for the needs and desires of others in the family is vital for any conflict[7]. In separating ourselves from overwhelming and emotional states during conflict, we can respond to the situation more wisely instead of perpetuating the projective identification cycles of getting rid of our ill-feeling by blaming others for it (see Chapter 1). Working with difficulty in this way shines a clearer light onto how we consider our own self. We hold self-attached, inwardly-looking mental constructs and thoughts about how we see ourselves, often caught in the labels of who we consider ourselves to be (whether parent, partner, son or daughter and so on). Later in the book we'll discuss how all challenges faced constitute a problem of the self, and during all family conflict it is how we relate to this difficulty through our idea of ourselves, and how we are affected, that limits and determines how we react or respond to what goes on. Acknowledging this on a moment by moment basis, creates an opportunity to come back to an attention on the self. From this automatic reactionary state of autopilot, we begin to naturally progress through the steps of awareness, attention, allowing and accepting. Then we are blessed with the option of making the best of our interactions within the family. We are all inclined towards making our mark, and imprinting what we hope to get out of life in the here and now on to those around us and those involved in our lives,. An obvious balance to realise is that we cannot expect everything to go our way all the time, and in a healthy family unit we need the space to allow each member to have their input.

Considering the mind and our negative states, most research focus has been on individuals rather than families and on pathology rather than health[8]. It's suggested that even in times of difficulty and confrontation then, there needs to be some balance of approaching situations and each other, with the idea that we need to first allow for the space to acknowledge that others have their own way of thinking, speaking and reacting within the same situation.

'Connecting before correcting'[9] is a common phrase for more effective family interactions, to make sure we establish a connection with each other before trying to influence a desired change in the thinking, speaking and actions of ourselves and our family members and trying to move towards more positive outcomes in those given circumstances. This is a great example of getting the better of our familial interactions, and transforming daily situations towards more positive outcomes. A good example is family life dominated by shouting and demanding, which is pretty common because we all have limited reserves of attention and energy. Usually when kids' actions need a bit of correcting for example, they're full of obstinacy and energy, and parents arc fatigued after long days spent parenting and managing other responsibilities of the busy, modern-day parent. Similarly, when partners are self-centred and challenging, patience and understanding are often the last solutions that come to mind! So it's comfortable to resort to the base-line, easy-to-implement methods of getting our cherished others to do as instructed, which more often than not means resorting to getting angrier, louder and feeling more deserving of having things go our way. Played out repetitively, this causes the obvious challenge that they'll continue to act as they do and we continue with the same actions out of mere habit. Family interaction can easily become habitually about getting upset, angry and frustrated, but not doing anything about it! Although this book is for awareness within the family at large, and not specifically about working with the mind from solely any individual perspective, this example shows quite nicely how to begin to use the process for improved outcomes and reduced harm within the family. This starts with noticing the challenge arising by, for example, a parent wishing their child to do as they are told. Perhaps this is observed as an awareness of frustration in the mind, and thoughts that may try to justify why the child should listen to the parent and what the parent needs from the obedience of the child in this situation (relief, quiet, rest, whatever). Perhaps there is an awareness of sensations in the body, a rising sensation, heightened sensitivity, tension or tightness in any group of muscles or the face, for example. This includes even awareness of our behaviour as the parent in this situation, noticing ourselves being or speaking in a threatening manner, becoming confrontational, or acting in a manner as affected and afflicted by the behaviour of our offspring.

Moving this state of mind to a less reactionary state involves some deliberate attention toward some opposite trigger to transform the suffering and negative outcomes through a positive frame of mind implemented in the same situation. This can be thought of as consciously relieving the pain of a situation that we were subconsciously engaged in (for both us and the family involved), by using a new neural pathway[10]. Put more simply, we think, speak or act deliberately to contradict what we were aware of as part of this challenging situation.

We will delve further into this idea of positive focus over the next couple of chapters. It's important in life to consider ways to deal with challenges because they are always there, and in noticing where we have the roots of limiting or negative reaction we can implement a change in how this affects us and the family around us. So, as we consider advancing our practice of working with the mind, this is nothing more than determining what we intend our change in ability to engage with life to be. It might be an improved ability to deal with a difficult parent or partner who perhaps has no interest in developing a wholesome relationship with us or our family. Or perhaps the ability to better hold back our own habits and characteristics that limit our ability to interact positively within the family. Or, it may simply be to make the most of our opportunity to self-develop and not self-limit – which is so easy to do unconsciously. Advancing our practice is where we use the benefits of a mindful outlook to improve our situation relative to our family experience. The choice to engage (even if only at a subconscious level) in some situation, or in dealing with some difficult aspect of the present through negative means, will more than likely lengthen the process of suffering involved in the situation. The conscious decision to engage in the same circumstance through a more open awareness, more positive outlook, or some means of having a frame of reference towards it being OK is wiser, despite more effort being needed to do this at first.

Even though we have considered consciousness itself as unscientific until fairly recently[11], we see now how conscious effort becomes easier to regulate and maintain, regardless of subconscious habits of reaction. So, changing the way that we are aware of, and place our attention when reacting to a situation is a transformation of a negative to positive state using the different states of the conscious mind. This can be thought of as 'training the brain', or better, noticing the 'inner talk' we have that contributes to or comes out of difficult situations[12].

Lack of communication is a common complaint for most families and in this sense we must listen if we expect to be heard[13], and notice in ourselves that which contributes to just wanting to talk (or await our turn to). If we can't bring ourselves to truly look at our own characteristics and habits of interaction first, expecting this of others cannot be justified. It may initially seem counter-intuitive to be opening up to any suffering involved in the family experience instead of turning away from it, especially where there is ongoing or severe difficulty in our present-moment experiences. So how do we then work towards being more able to make that choice, especially if the decisions surrounding how we pay attention to challenge are usually made under autopilot, highly-charged or emotional situations, or where we have little time to interact with family more carefully? Where our concepts of who we are and how things should be influence an entrenched point of view of getting rid of what we don't like about this situation, this desire to change how things unfold will always have a negative focus. Advancing a positive state of mind to counteract this starts with intention – where we decide to work with the mind and observe a mindful space of awareness. This enables our subconscious habitual reactions to progressively become more inclined towards the positive even if the situation is negative[14]. This is a balanced state of mind, often referred to as being equanimous (calm and composed), or knowing equanimity and balance in our approaches. This doesn't mean that we ignore or never experience the emotions of life, just that in our approaches we know we can come back to a baseline-settled state of mind more easily, and not get as lost in the cycling of emotions that arise[15]. **Figure 4.1** below is a representation of some recent research findings that can further support this idea.

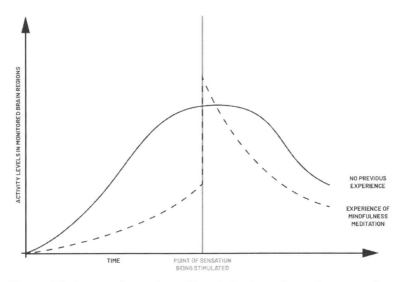

Figure 4.1 - Comparison of reactions in brain regions of non-medi-tators and those experienced in mindfulness practices

Scans of the brain were conducted on experienced practitioners of mindfulness-based practices and a control group who had not practised before, measuring activity of the brain. Participants were subjected to an expected 'unwanted sensation', such as heat or a pin prick but were not told exactly when this would be. The brain activity of those with experience of mindfulness was more realistic to the situation, having a sharp response to the stimulus, and a quick return to no activity afterwards. The brains of those who hadn't any experience of aware-ness and attention practice showed a different activity, already beginning to react to the situation long before the sensation was stimulated, and taking much longer for the brain activity to subside after the event[16]. The experience of working with the mind changes the brain, such that we are less inclined to live experiences that are actually not there, or get caught up in associated emotion and memory rather than remain present and responsive to the people and places that we are in.

Letting go of the natural inhibition we all have surrounding things of the mind is an impressive feat, helped by working with our intention, which may seem strange at first. Chapter 8 will provide some clarity and guidance on this. Fundamentally our intention can be thought of as our road map. If we set off in a planned direction having taken precautions to establish how and why we should get there, we're more likely to arrive at the desired destination. Looking to get rid of and to move away from our immediate suffering as soon as possible, comes naturally from the inherent perspective that we shouldn't have to experience negativity (something we'll look at in the next chapter). It's natural to not want to feel bad, but we can come to notice when this itself causes an imbalance in our state of mind, and that actually it's realistic to expect suffering and difficulty in life. This is neither a pessimism nor a pragmatism, it merely allows for awareness of whatever comes while still maintaining some equanimity. It's far more productive to move our mind to the how and why of situations that challenge us, and away from what effect this has on us (how we feel and are inclined to react because of this).

For advancing our working with the mind we don't need to know all the answers to our life challenges, or ways out of our difficult states of mind, we just need to reflect on and come to know that this is just part of that present-moment experience of life. By allowing this experience to be OK as it is, and to accept that it is just experience, we may in time come to an appreciation of difficulty as part of the journey we must undergo for this transformation towards a more positive outlook and intent in life[17]. It's important to know that if we want things in life to change, we have to change things in life. This change includes the way we allow ourselves to think, speak and act. These form the very basis of our habitual response patterns, which in turn affect the outcomes of our day-to-day family life. Looking with enough honesty and subtlety, we see that how we think about, talk to and behave towards other people in the family is a significant prediction of family outcomes; and how we have greater control over our thinking, speaking and acting when we chose to! This realisation begs the question – why do we not all influence a greater change for positive outcomes more often, by working with ourselves and our awareness and then extending this outward to all situations? Change like this is a gradual process, and at the level of society and the individual, it's easy to overlook what we can achieve and change in a year, then similarly to expect too much significant development in a mere few weeks. Change within oneself is the only real thing we can focus on to instigate a change within our surroundings and family unit, and to make any difference, on whatever scale our intention is. Whether we aim to try and curb our own harmful idiosyncrasies, better allow and accept other people's, or encourage and support family to be able to do this themselves, this process is the same development – firstly of the self then extending this outwards.

This gradual process requires us not to have any unrealistic expectations, because these leave us feeling deflated and downtrodden about the process of change when it isn't as instant as we would like. Where we hold onto pleasant experiences or ideas of what should happen in practice, we risk becoming needlessly disappointed when exercises don't conform to these expectations[18] which sets us up for further limitations. Expectations of instant gratification actively perpetuate some of the most harmful states of mind a person can have. We need only look at our own impatience and that of those around us to see this. Fuelled by the instant-response, easily-obtained intoxication, technologically comforting and distracting world we live in, many of us today find it scary, mysterious or even offensive to reflect on true meaning or purpose in our routine lives[19]. Anything to snap us out of the autopilot state of normal routines and frames of mind, of 'going through the motions', is powerful when thinking about implementing new routines. This should always be remembered as a process and not an end point. Starting with an awareness of the current status quo, we can then work on breaking that automatic thinking and conditioning, with a view to having that space of awareness or frame of mind replaced by another, that is seeing the current situation as something more than it is through a more proactive perspective. A way of looking at it as being something that is to be of benefit rather than just another day. Einstein noted that everything is miraculous or that nothing is, depending on our individual perception, and this is a powerful idea to keep in mind whilst considering what benefits we get from working with the mind and how to advance this practice.

A united front is important when moving forward as a family unit, in progressing the current stages of our relationships within the family, and in working towards and realising our family plans, whatever these may be. This is equally as important for coming to a clearer understanding and experience of ourselves, and how 'who we are' and our values result in how we react to familiar family situations and in response to the behaviour of others in our family unit. Challenges in family life are more-or-less always present, in one area or another in different forms and intensities, so establishing a good, mindful awareness of ourselves and family life helps enormously. Subtle, scalable and significant effect arises out of a regular, concentrated effort to include more positive interaction within the family setting. This is true whether it is taking the time to think of something nice a partner may appreciate, or showing some active attention to a family member that we feel could do with showing us more positive attention. It's easy and very common for us to share some of our negative self with those closest to us, because our interactions with them are so frequent, it becomes familiar and automatic[20]. We often focus less on how to keep this interaction constructive, especially when compared with how we're more naturally inclined to do this with new people and unfamiliar settings.

A good example is of active listening, and actually being present and hearing how and why someone in the family is expressing themselves. This is something that we'd expect from them for ourselves, and showing respectful, attentive focus to what is being thought, said and enacted is useful[21]. Even where we disagree with, don't care for, or disapprove of what's being expressed, the allowing and accepting of it is key! It is a much more affirming process than just idly waiting to throw in our point of view or opinion on what's being expressed. Even if the person is express- ing criticism, we see what happens when this is met with a positive open mind and intent, just by hearing and not reacting[22]. It's easy to expect this of others, and to point out the flawed and negative ways they do things. However, this disclosure itself becomes a negative experience, and we are best served by turning this attention on ourselves, for we too behave imperfectly. The mind's tendency to focus quite naturally on the negative or difficult tends to mean that when we look at, deal with, or react to such challenge or intent for positive change, it's often from a frame of mind governed by this focus on the negative (and usually aimed outwardly at others). Our perspective on things, or at least our immediate subconscious reaction and state of mind arising in response to events, is deter- mined largely by our desire and our energy. So delving into this a little helps us to notice a negative autopilot state as it occurs.

This will become more familiar to us as we notice our- selves wanting, not wanting, being tired, agitated or indif- ferent. This is the way the mind tends to categorise things, highlighting the often natural tendency we have towards the negative which comes about as we see for ourselves that we desire more of things that we like, and less of things we don't. We see ourselves as being too tired, or not having enough energy and motivation to do things in life that are outside our comfort zone. Or we reflect on being too busy and hectic, with too many responsibilities to be calm enough or able to take account of ourselves mind- fully. In between these apathetic and agitated states is where we just tend to feel an indifference, when we don't particularly want anything nor are we worked up or unmotivated about something. So in attempting to change what is some aspect of family life we may wish to improve upon, we look at it from the perspective that the situation isn't what it should be! This is less empowering than from a differing perspective which is appreciative of what we can learn from the situation, or how we can look at it differently for desired or improved outcomes or towards minimising harm in more extreme situations. Where we pay attention to the pain involved in life, we continue to suffer, but where we pay attention to the opportunity and lesson offered we can begin to grow, using this suffering as fertiliser for the growth process[23].

Within the family unit it's useful to notice in others this tendency of the mind towards a negative focus, seeing the habitual ways of reacting to situations, sensations, thoughts and subsequent speaking and actions. All too often we overlook the fact that the others in our family also face challenge and difficulty, and that our relationships with them are variable and not absolute[24]. Even where we see ourselves as the one trying to hold a family together and that seemingly the others don't, or ourselves as right and others as wrong, even here they still suffer and we cannot expect our happiness and well-being to be their responsibilty[25]. We are ultimately all in the game of family life resulting from our own intention, and with greater awareness we come to see more openly the intentions of ourselves and others. Consider for a moment what this means for our efforts in addressing family needs, however significant or small, instead of individually addressing our desires through the family platform. If we do indeed even allow such focus to take precedence over other areas of life, as we are all inclined to just allow our attention to waiver between whatever arises each day. We're likely to see that much of the time we're engaged in reacting to situations moment by moment, rather than being more openly aware of or responding to each and noticing honestly where our intentions lie. There's something intriguing about the habitual, natural way that we tend to go through the day automatically, often only realising after events when the mind is clear of the emotion, and immediate cognitive processing of what's arising that we could have, should have or will next time respond differently or more appropriately. Yet mostly, we don't do this.

There is something comforting about the status quo of the mind, which can feel unnerving to alter and develop through working with the mind. Urgency in this is very real as we come to face the languorous, depleting energy of wavering attention more openly. There's a subtle difference in observing how we react, and what we think, feel and say whilst reacting. It's only after establishing greater awareness to be able to observe this more clearly, that we may be able to consider how we may react, think, feel or speak differently in an effort to alter our circumstances and outcomes. So really, all this working with 'mind stuff' or practice is only about a few things, but used in different contexts to illicit a positive transformation or change. Fundamentally, all we do is focus on a few things, starting with establishing an awareness of paying attention in the present moment, which means we are being deliberately mindful and focused on something. By looking in more depth through greater attention at one element of the many that combine to make the present moment, the option to change our present moment perspective becomes more immediately accessible[26]. When we begin to put this into place with some comfort, repetition, familiarity or confidence, we see the results of when our attention is continually and automatically divided. Especially so whilst in this context, when we're running through the motions and emotions of family life, it's very easy to be doing one task with minimal attention. Others fly through our minds at the same time, and whilst we engage in one thing our thoughts and attention are often elsewhere.

When we consider the responsibility involved in running the home, maintaining good family relationships, getting parents to listen and understand, and encouraging kids to be more, do more and help out more, there is a lot involved. It's no wonder the mind multitasks! Seemingly, nothing would ever get done if we didn't think about many things at once, and the ability to pay attention to different things *is* important in life, no doubt. Deliberate attention is a remarkable tool however, as we see in Chapters 3, 6 and 9 of this book. Working with the mind actually increases our ability to pay attention to different and difficult things in life, and to be consciously aware when this is overwhelming, whilst enabling us to reduce much of the suffering and harm this can cause when left to the subconscious, unaware mind. With practice we are better equipped to deal with difficult situations[27], and can develop our ability to embody how our family members can become a bit more resilient to the ebb and flow of emotional energy that they naturally experience in response to circumstances and situations in life.

Deliberate attention doesn't mean we become robotic, single-track minded and incapable of managing the many tasks we must complete each day. However, it does mean we can choose where to place our efforts, attention and energy, resulting in a gradual increase in being able to influence our own frame of mind. In a remarkably short space of time we come to see the value this has on our immediate life context, efforts and endeavours throughout the day. When emotions are high, time is short and the pressure is on to resolve some situation or other, our state of mind is likely to be predominantly governed by automatic focus on the negative. For example, we see how annoying it is that our wishes and preferences are overlooked when others aren't listening. We feel frustrated that we want to help them see our perspective but they don't, or won't understand, and we can't get the point across effectively to them. We are easily frustrated or angered at such situations and, as people continue to act contrary to our desires, undermining our sense of self or our control, our resolve dissolves and we have no perspective except for that of the immediate difficulty. It's understood that some level of such stressful functioning can be beneficial[28], but also that the effects of fight, flight or freeze responses can be crippling. Where we are constantly losing tempers and yelling we may actually be inducing nothing but a temporary mental paralysis, rather than getting ourselves understood[29]! It's more straightforward for us to focus in on the difficulty, frustration and hurt, than to learn what this means about that particular situation and how we could have tried to balance getting it to go our way a little more positively.

Changing perspective is the only way of interacting with all situations differently, no matter our place in the family or what happens, because much of life is beyond our personal power to change. Shattering the generally self-negative ways this manifests is revolutionary on many levels. We may not be able to get other family members to listen and understand, because generally people have no (or very limited capacity) to empathise with what's outside of them! However, from a more positive and able frame of mind, we will do a much better job at getting our point across without being left with, or passing on, as much of a negative focus. Re-framing the mind this way takes practice, because we so naturally and powerfully view the things that challenge us as something that needs to change, and not as something we can change the way we look at or engage with. The baby crying in the middle of the night is no different to a 4-year-old screaming for more TV, or our kids' and teens' self-centred woes when all we want is peace, quiet and rest, some brief hiatus to the catering to, cleaning-up after and coming down from the madness involved in forever following this pattern. There's little time in all this to take account of the kind of parent, partner or family member we have become, and to notice our responses when our loved ones are testing our limits. Families that have strategies in place for staying cool, for taking time to take account of their relationships, individual needs and being a couple of steps ahead of the game by not resorting to screaming at each other all the time, are not families free of difficulty, challenge and confrontation. Even these relationships are strained, and despite perhaps the surface appearance of together-ness, people still do not see eye-to-eye all the time.

Families that successfully account for each other just have a method in place of reviewing such situations, learn-ing from them, trying and implementing ideas and solutions to mitigating, controlling or managing these challenges more positively. Ability to do this always comes back to first better managing our own emotional triggers[30], and working with the mind is something that helps us underpin such efforts and values. Through this process we and our family are likely to be far more aware of the boundaries we have as a group, to have an improved awareness of our-selves as individuals and to have a greater appreciation of each other (especially in trying situations). Even in the most acrimonious of family set-ups, where the status quo is quite challenging by the very nature of the relationships of the family unit alone, there is great benefit to being able to implement this skill set (like damage control, and mini-mising harm).

Remembering the sheer scale of the spectrum of humanity for a moment, it's no surprise that families func-tion differently, and some perhaps by comparison to our ideal, do so in a dysfunctional way. The same process is entirely true of our relationships to each other as parents and care-givers: some awareness of the challenges we confront as individuals, and as couples, is extremely pow-erful when building our strengths as a family unit. Self-development may be a little bit of an overused platitude, but is definitely something we all overlook most of the time, *and is key if we wish our family to grow* or to mitigate the suffering of difficult family situations.

Consider for a moment the values a parent may wish to instil in their children. Openness, honesty respectfulness, politeness, diligence, fearlessness and balance perhaps (just some examples of virtuous attributes)? Whatever our wishes for our kids, they most certainly don't pick up values from merely being told, 'calm down', 'do as you're told', 'just listen to me', 'be yourself', or whatever we tell them time and time again. People learn from observing, and listening is just one aspect thereof. How we think, speak and act has a far greater influence than just telling family and others what to do. Unfortunately or not, 'do as I say, not as I do' doesn't go very far in today's world[31]. Dorothy Law Nolte put it marvellously in 'Children Learn What They Live' in the poem adapted here.

Children living with criticism learn to condemn
Living with hostility, they learn to fight
With fear, to be apprehensive
With pity, to feel sorry for them-self
With ridicule, to be shy
With jealousy, to feel envy
With shame, to feel guilty
BUT
If a child lives with tolerance, they learn to be patient
With encouragement, they learn to be confident
With praise, to be appreciative
With acceptance, to love
With approval, to like themselves
With honesty, they learn what truth is
With fairness, they learn justice
If children live with recognition, they learn to have a goal.

If children live with sharing, they learn to be generous.
If a child lives with security, they learn to have faith in
them-self and those about them
If a child lives with friendliness, they learn the world is a
nice place in which to live.

Not all of us are fortunate enough to have been raised in a family embracing this ideal, or to be in a position to do so for those we raise, because this takes a lot of self-knowledge and self-sacrifice! So, when we wish the rest of our family to be open and honest, we must be open and honest with them, and they will observe us embodying the example of that which we desire to experience in the family unit. This can come from them observing us open up and share, or come clean and speak truth to something or some situation we'd rather not be transparent about – both are probably something we don't do enough. Where our family sees us go through the discomfort of this openness, it is far more powerful than allowing the subconscious familiarity of not taking some accountability for our issues as individuals, that impact upon the rest of the family unit32.

Allowing others to witness situations in our own lives that are emotional and overwhelming for us and talking openly, and age-appropriately about these is no mean feat. This is true even within our immediate family, as there is the natural desire to seem stable, OK and strong, which we feel will be undermined if we are to open enough to allow our loved ones to see our low points. Perhaps this stems from the lack of a significantly deeper self-awareness, because after we regularly observe ourselves through the open-minded filter of a heightened awareness, we see that true stability and strength comes from embracing and allowing ourselves to see our imbalance and weakness – not ignoring it. If we continually look away, we cannot do anything to develop our current self and progress, but such avoidance is hard-wired!

We are often inclined not to enable this opportunity for our kids, families and even ourselves to reflect on challenge and its effect. We naturally turn away from obstacles and difficult frames of mind, somehow believing, even if only subconsciously, that we shouldn't suffer from or have to learn to cope with such things, or to have to look at them directly. This belief persists even though doing so can actually offer greater clarity[33]. However, and here's the point, where we would prefer those we interact with would have greater life skills such as listening, caring, patience, tolerance, respect, diligence all the good stuff in life – we may have to start with ourselves (we are key to our own experiences after all!). We must find some way of observing opportunity to learn these skills from life experiences, and to interrupt the naturally automatic mind on occasion. This means looking inwardly at some level to see the perceived weaknesses and natural inclination we have to resort to frustration, anger and so on. If we don't see this in ourselves, we must look with a clearer mind. For it is in recognising and working with such aspects of the self that enables us to interact with, and embody, more powerful and positive values. It is our own self-distraction that is the cause of our difficulties and so, even in conflict with others, it is ourselves that we must look at, and develop our family in this way. Where our family members or others have very little intention to develop, learn, change and treat themselves or others more positively, these skills will at least ensure we don't kill ourselves trying to get them to. We're less likely to be so negatively affected by harsh situations, and the outlooks and actions of others that afflict us, once we have some grasp of this through working with the mind. We see the subtle interplay of the characteristics of ourselves and others, as a changing state of emotions and frames of mind all determining the resulting thoughts, words and actions. We also see more of the positive intention that benefits us in our own thinking, speaking and behaviour. Where we desire patience, tolerance, respect and diligence, for example, we begin to allow ourselves to notice the innate impatience, intolerance, disrespect and laziness in ourselves. Most of us don't like looking at our own flaws, or perceived weaknesses for too long. In fact, the topic of the self is something most of us don't allow ourselves the luxury of investigating at all! It is progressively less something frowned upon in the march of today's world towards being more open-minded about things, but still less usual for most of us to experience greater awareness in ourselves.

Now, here's the interesting part: allowing ourselves the self-enquiry to be honest enough to know our own values, our own short-comings, our own character flaws and skill deficits begins to make it easier to allow the shortcomings of others without such immediate results such as being as emotionally affected. In the more traditional sense, the purpose of motivating ourselves towards greater self-awareness is the compassion for ourselves and others in life34 that we'll come on to in Chapter 7.

The process of being a part of a family is itself a process of development. Whether intended or not, we are faced with a whole set of unforeseen challenges. A few months can seem a lifetime of change during the lives of our kids as we watch each progressive development, then the challenges we face change all over again and we're confronted with an entirely new state of normal! If we do not allow the time for ourselves as individuals and collectives within a family to come to an awareness of who we are, how we present ourselves, and in what ways we habitually react to the world around us, we will be ill-prepared to guide and support successive generations in this practice of self-awareness. We must do unto ourselves as we'd like others to do unto themselves! Reflect for a moment on the scale and significance of the effects this could have, considering that in the UK alone there are over 19 million families35! This working with the mind through Attention, Awareness, Allowing, Accepting, Acknowledging, Advancing and then (as we'll get to in the next chapter) Appreciating, comes from a progressive self-realisation that enables us to look more clearly at experience, duty and responsibility. Without such practice we leave ourselves prone to succumbing to the inevitable stresses and challenges presented by our responsibilities of family and everyday life.

Thoughts about family need to be turned on their head, for example there's so much planning and thinking about the ideal wedding, lavish birth and beautiful house, compared with the effort and attention placed on wholesome marriage, healthy upbringing and happy home life, that many of our families are naturally destined to fall apart. We plan for what makes us feel good, and not as often for how we will fill the space in between these feel-good events. Although there's nothing wrong with focus on the positive and beautiful, it is unrealistic to assume family life (and life generally) will bear no burdens. Life will test and strike fear into us at times, and proactively considering and facing this is important in overcoming it[36]. Family breakdown is fine, where its members (especially the kids) are supported to realise and arrive at the most effective way of going through what they must, to become who they will. This is perhaps not always an obvious or easy thing to do.

Although, slightly aside from the topic of this content, it's perhaps useful to draw attention momentarily to the significance of family life, and of developing a united front capable of weathering the inevitable storms of family conflict (even where this may mean planning for the most appropriate end to a family unit that's become toxic or unsustainable.) If this means ultimately minimising harm for a particular family, then all the better for that family. Remembering that we learn from what we observe not just what we are told, so maintaining a destructive status quo to save face never results in stability for our minds – young or old.

Planning home life and not just thinking about a nice home, having good intention and thinking about parenting and not just designing the ideal birth, and considering how we can bring ourselves to sustain a loving, wholesome life with partners, and not just dreaming up beautiful weddings is the united front. It is giving of ourselves, knowing we are but one element of the family unit, being aware of the desires, needs, inclinations and preferences of the other members of our family. This shifting away from the

'I' perspective is hard for many ("it's my child and I'll raise him/her how I want") when thinking or speaking about a person who is individual and separate to who we are. It is never our child owned and controlled, merely the child over whom we have the momentary privilege of authority *and responsibility* to show and guide as best we can[37]. The same applies for thoughts of 'my' partner or parents, 'my' relationship, for these are things beyond the self alone. Asserting ownership, being controlling and I-focused assumes authority but overlooks responsibility, because we must forgo the self and look outside of 'I' for skills, knowledge and support from the partner, family unit or others, to learn to show and guide as befits the need of family as a whole. 'I' doesn't have skills, knowledge or ability by itself, which are sufficient to manage a healthy, wealthy, happy family unit (we will cover more about 'I' and the concept of the self in the second half of the book). Family, specifically, is greater than 'I', because 'we' is needed for family to even begin. Deeply ingrained I-focus is natural, and we can overcome our conditioned minds through simple practice, as we'll allude to throughout the book. If this seems repetitive, consider that to know and not to do, is to not know at all. If we do not use the knowledge (understanding and experience) that we have, it is of no real use!

All family members can act and react in habit-forming ways that are unhelpful or unhealthy for overall family dynamics, therefore allowing for each other is important. Extending our awareness to an appreciation of the limitations of others, as well as ourselves, is vital for family balance. Knowing that our partner struggles as much as (or even more than we do) with a certain aspect of the home life or parenting requirements, is an opportunity to extend our love and support. As is the realisation of our need for support and the opportunity to seek it from another. Knowing that children attempt to make sense of unintelligible experience and emotion in their minds on a daily basis, coming to grips with themselves, body, mind and the world they live in is vast and confusing. These are painful, or at least uncomfortable, realisations when we delve into allowing awareness of our self, because we may not always be the kind of person we internally automatically assume and reassure ourselves to be. Although this book in the series is not specifically about relationship advice or guidance, the information contained leans largely on the need for a stable relationship foundation or base for the family. This is far more important than the specific structure of our family because there is no family set-up or required characteristics, gender or sexuality of the parent(s) that makes for a more successful family than others[38].

Stability in oneself first always greatly enables this in the family at large. Self-stability requires us to reach out of and beyond our current self-concept. In Chapter 5 we look into direct ways of implementing this. The six steps for working with the mind introduced so far – if nothing else at this point – should make us realise one thing: that we always have the option of coming back to this idea of a process of change – changing our focus to connect with a better intention, regardless of our present experience. Where we're aware of something negative or difficult which may make us feel awkward or uncomfortable, we can transform the state of mind we're in as we're involved in this situation. The challenge of anything in life that's hard is largely in the interpretation of the situation or circumstance we find ourselves in, and we tend to regard the situation itself as the problem[39]. We're hard-wired to over-react before we can respond wisely, to worry about what's outside of our influence to control, and to avoid that which is hard for us. There are no true facts about family life, just our interpretations of the information presented to us by the current focus of the mind. All these things further disturb the mind, and so how do we find an alternative? Over the next few chapters we'll progressively delve into another, more positive approach.

Appreciation

Healing is a matter of time, but it is also
sometimes a matter of opportunity.

eeing the world around us with more appreciation can remove much of the stress and strain of constantly seeking the outcomes that we want to achieve, and often, makes reaching our goals more rewarding as we work towards them. Gratitude is a value that can be effectively practised to help us see the beauty in life, and to appreciate the simple things around us regardless of our position in life, or our sense of ourselves (our self-concept). We will now introduce the idea of looking at our day-to-day activities with more gratefulness, then also look at how we all naturally tend to want to avoid unpleasant experiences in life, because they result in strong or negative emotions. We'll learn how to alter this tendency by working with the mind. This then helps us to accept all negative aspects of life as they occur, without being judgmental. Positive anchors are powerful antidotes to negative thoughts and emotions, as we'll come to see, but for now we're focused here on generating a thankful appreciation for both that which is positive and negative. Both are part of our life experience, even if in our concept of ourselves we overlook the negative, or that which we don't like about ourselves and our experiences.

The world around us has become incredibly materialistic – which we should not think of as being fundamentally right or wrong in and of itself – and whatever we yearn for, whether it is for more money, a better lifestyle, designer clothes, the latest mobile phone, or a new car, all these are perfectly acceptable. If we are leading a life where we have reasonable health, a roof over our head, and food to eat, we're already in a better place than most. This is where appreciation comes into its own, because we *all* have seemingly insignificant things to be grateful for in life and, ironically, it's our opinions and the habitual way we come to think about life which leads us to taking it for granted. We never have absolutely *nothing* to be grateful for, it's just that we've been conditioned to never take the time to be truly grateful, and have forgotten how powerful this is. We often desire more, which is not a negative thing in itself, because desire is key to triggering our motivation and drive to develop, grow and live. We also needn't get caught up here in thinking about materialism, or even in opposing it either, we just simply need to notice the disparity between need and desire – and be aware of how we fundamentally assume they're the same! It's important that we develop a heightened ability to be aware of our desires, however. We need to take note when we are assuming that wanting more is a sure way of having a better or happier life, or when our desires are actually a path to suffering (which, when left unobserved, they very often are). We tend to get stuck in the loop: "I will be happy when I obtain that, achieve that, when such and such happens". Of course, when these things do indeed happen, the mind races to the next set of goals, ambitions and targets. Now desire is very important if we want to stay motivated and not land up with no ambition in life, but we must stop thinking that our success and happiness are only based on achievement. If this were true then deep and meaningful happiness would be forever elusive because achievement is not an absolute. In other words, we achieve different things throughout life, some immediately and others progressively. Practising gratitude can be a key element of this process of working towards positive things in life, whilst remaining unaffected by however the journey unfolds.

This way we see happiness isn't linked to our desires, and we avoid the situation where the negative experience of not getting what we want outweighs the positive intent behind why we desire it to begin with. If we're not careful, the constant striving to achieve more, get more, or have more, without being grateful for what we already have, can have quite devastating effects on family life! We lose sight of the present moment through life's distractions, and miss seeing the good that is happening in our lives right now, because we're lost in the craving for things that may not be part of our present experience. Working with the mind comes to our rescue here, and mindfully focusing on the present underpins all of the practical exercises we'll come to in the next few chapters. As we become more focused on feeling grateful, we can feel more connected to each other, and appreciate the value of the experiences that we do have. We can even be grateful that there is conflict in our lives, so that we can practice learning more open-minded approaches to dealing with people and situations we struggle to positively relate to. The idea of mindfulness-based practices and modern approaches to open the mind to these means of finding gratefulness, have developed over time. In the box below is a brief overview of this development, and the current standards for practitioners and teachers of mindfulness-based programmes.

Mindfulness-based stress reduction (MBSR), developed in the 1970s by Jon Kabat-Zinn and his team at the University of Massachusetts Medical Centre, is hailed as the programme that started the process of mindfulness-based theory and practice becoming more available, understandable and acceptable to the modern and more Western frame of mind. Kabat-Zinn's attempts were largely focused on the reduction of pain and suffering, specifically for those with various conditions or lifestyle challenges that were difficult to treat conventionally in a hospital setting. The use of MBSR in the hospital setting in 1979 provided the first controlled clinical research into mindfulness practice. Mindfulness-based cognitive therapy, or MBCT, was a development which arose in the 1990s out of the work of clinical psychologists Mark Williams, John Teasdale and Zindel Segal, who all studied Kabat-Zinn's MBSR programme. Their experimentation was specifically centred on depression, and the prevention of the recurrence of depression, all subject to research and review. Their work built upon the emergence of new concepts of the mind, including a metacognitive awareness, or an ability to experience thoughts and feelings as mental events that pass through the mind – and not to experience them as part of the self.

This model of the mind is closely linked to the more religious and traditional teachings that Kabat-Zinn incorporated into MBSR, which considers thoughts and feelings to be impermanent, and objective matters in the moment-by-moment awareness of the mind. Some brief information on the religious and spiritual nature of working with the mind is available in **Appendix 2) Standards and origins**, because each faith tradition has its origins in the enquiry into self, but actually, this need not be of any real concern to us here. It is easier to get caught up in noticing what is different about ourselves, our faiths or lack thereof, than to reflect on our similarities and how, despite our differing beliefs, we all have the same needs. Development of the use of mindfulness in the English-speaking world has emerged over the last few decades of adaptations born of these early clinical interventions, with mindfulness practice now much more heavily reported on, available to study and being accessible as part of a wider range of services and programmes. In some countries there are minimum industry standards in place today, because of the emergence of the professional context and demand for mindfulness services, so as to ensure that those offering such services are suitably trained and experienced.

Expressing gratitude for that which we do have in life, whether it be things, people, memories, or anything else, leads to increased happiness when included as part of a routine practice[1]. Research in this area suggests it improves health and well-being in many ways, and that we can do this by speaking or thinking gratefully, by acting thankfully or even finding ways to reflect gratitude in mindfulness practice or writing letters[2]. It may feel strange when we deliberately start to address the thought stream to seek something positive to be grateful for, and some of us may find it difficult at first. There needn't be grand gestures of appreciation to begin with, just simple thoughts of being thankful for something small, like a glass of water when we're thirsty or the food we have to eat when we're hungry. The marvel and intricacy of life can easily be appreciated in the small, easily overlooked aspects of it which we take for granted each day, and pay little or no attention to. Even a thing as simple as a glass of water is a powerful means of transformation, if we see it through the altered filter of perspective in greater awareness, with our attention focused on appreciation. We usually just drink it, without paying any real attention to detail or exercising a deliberate, heightened awareness of the situation, and certainly without focus on the significance of it[3]. Such is true for most of us in many of life's situations – we're on autopilot and missing something much grander.

This isn't to say that there is some specific way of becoming happier, free of suffering and the trials of the ups and downs of family life. However, we begin to glimpse some aspect of ourselves through working with the mind, and we see that this happiness, and freedom from suffering is intrinsic, already in us no matter how challenging life is right now. In this sense there isn't anything that we specifically have to do to achieve happiness in family life, no programme plan or steps to follow that help us achieve the state of happiness. We can come to look at our habitual self, and more openly notice how we pave the way to our own difficulty. This may sit awkwardly for some of us, so it may help to consider that happiness is not an absolute, and is highly dependent on our outlook. In any given moment our feelings of happiness have little to do with our family, or our conditions, and more to do with our perception of it, and how satisfied we are with what we have[4]. In this regard, our concept of our self and our family interactions are extremely important, as we come to view ourselves and relationships progressively more openly and alter this perspective. Appreciation is a helpful tool in changing our state of mind towards this thinking. There is a greater confidence and stability that comes as we reach outside of our current concept of the self. This is something that feeds powerfully into our self-esteem and resilience as a person which, in turn, supports our family and the challenges and conflicts that happen as part of family life. In time we may come to see much of what happens in life as something precious, and worth appreciating.

Gratitude is a powerful tool to bring positivity to our lives, and as we become more grateful, this links strongly to increased well-being in our lives[5]. We may appreciate relationships with others better (the good and the bad), rather than taking them for granted. Remember that feelings of ups and downs are inherent in life, and know that a key principle of working with the mind is such that both pleasant and unpleasant experiences need to be observed and treated on equal terms. This is another idea that may seem a little unusual on the surface, because why would we deliberately pay attention to, then come to allow, accept or try to appreciate the awful things that happen in our lives and those situations and circumstances that really test us? Determining what's good or bad is based on how we habitually wish for happiness and freedom from suffering; nobody intrinsically wants the good *and* the bad! By this reasoning alone all that's inside the mind and that happens to us externally can be seen as equal, when viewed as a necessary part of what makes us who we are whilst realising greater self awareness[6].

Negative emotion is a natural part of life[7], but it also destroys our happiness, so this doesn't mean that we needn't do anything about it – how we find balance by responding more wisely to this is key. Gratitude can become a platform from which this balance is easier to strike. Including how a focus on gratitude in our routine observance of working with the mind can help interrupt the subconscious pattern of avoiding troubles that we may be facing in our lives. "Acknowledging the good already in life is the foundation for all abundance"[8] aptly describes the beginning of the process of starting to feel less overwhelmed by the seemingly bad aspects of life, and how powerful appreciation practices can be, whether we seek a happier family, less personal suffering or anything else.

When things don't go our way or we don't get what we want, we're often unhappy. Yet often when we do get these things, we then need more to stay happy because we instinctively are focused outside of the present, on what we don't want to lose, don't have or used to have. In this sense both achievement and possessions are poor indicators of lasting happiness and family status because once obtained they quickly become the past, and we then look for something else to strive towards[9]. The mind seems to be geared towards basking in pleasurable experiences and glossing over unpleasant moments. This sense of avoiding what feels 'bad' and expecting to feel 'good' too often can lead to negative, self-limiting habits which are difficult to break. This can make it tough for us to live in the present moment, not distractedly, and enjoy the moments of life, as there often seems something inherently uncomfortable and unhelpful to us about just being in the present moment. We think about and try to control and plan everything, stay in a distracted state keeping the mind incessantly busy – then subsequently we may not see negative states of mind arising, developing and becoming habit. The moment we stop over-thinking and aiming to control everything and remaining distracted, we can enjoy this very moment (whatever is arising in our experience) and things will automatically start settling. This can be unnerving in itself for those of us so deeply entrenched in our current states of mind. By observing this settled state we will not need to keep avoiding the here and now, the stillness in which our intuitive voice of calm, and the paradoxical empty fullness of everything exists.

The pattern of addiction is a good example to compare this avoidance tendency with. As an addict (even if just to our coffee or habitual emotions) we know that the routine use of whatever particular stimulant or intoxicant we favour may be harmful on some level, but this is preferred to the state of not being influenced by it, because it feels helpful or normal. Knowledge is theoretical, and the use of a substance is practical, experiential and where it is experienced routinely enough, becomes part of the habitual, subconscious experience and frame of reference in life. When we have to face periods without our favoured compounds to get us through the day, we can find the experience to be quite overwhelming! Similarly, when the noisy, distracted mind doesn't self-observe, what difficulties that can create for us! When we self-observe we see the states of mind which contribute to our individuality more clearly, including where these contribute towards and compound situations that are overwhelming in terms of our emotional states and experiences, often resulting in further thought, speech or action that is self limiting or harmful to those we care about.

The subconscious mind deals most routinely with what is fed through the mind consciously first, so on reflection the addicted mind may think 'I don't want this anymore' and yet not be able or ready to just stop. Until this decision for change has become established in the subconscious, this choice to stop whatever addictive tendency we may have, will likely be supplanted by the habitual decisions already there. This is similar to the avoider, when seeking pleasure, hiding from difficulty, and disassociating from the present in the mind. The key is to try to remain consciously present with dissatisfaction, to observe challenge and keep the mind focused on task often enough so that it can interrupt some of the more limiting subconscious patterns. We're all avoiders to some extent or other, and the impact this has on our relationship with the self and with loved ones are always harmful at some level. It's argued the key to a happy and peaceful life is to avoid all forms of avoidance and distraction. This isn't to say that we must have no care for the past or future, never make plans and only be concerned with what's under our noses all the time. Nothing would ever get done if this were true, and we should be wary of unknowingly (or perhaps deliberately) use mindful states of mind as further means of disassociating, or as an excuse to avoid having to do things.

Mindfulness is all about *accepting* – accepting emotions as they arise without being judgemental, and instead of running away from struggles in life, embracing them. Of course, this all starts with being aware of them. If we're not conscious of how we feel most of the time there's little we can do about it! Consciousness itself is interesting, and although modern science doesn't yet have an adequately refined method of investigating this fully[10], through working with the mind we can gain much more of a personal understanding and experience of greater conscious awareness (and the benefits this has for us and our family). By appreciating things as they are, instead of how we planned or would prefer them to be, many difficulties in life lose much of their power to sway our emotions[11]. This isn't to say that we have no control when working with the mind, or that we should give up our control and never do anything. However, we can strengthen an intuitive state using mindfulness-based tools to help us notice when what we're focused on isn't where our attention is needed, then to bring the mind to task and out of autopilot and avoidance.

In many cases avoidance can become quite detrimental over time, inhibit our basic enjoyment of family life, contribute to anxiety, stress, depression (or other negative states) and stop us from progressing or excelling in life at all. Opening up the inhibited mind through appreciation of what is there, even in a negative present-moment experience of life, helps us face challenges in life all the better and prevents us from unloading our woes so frequently onto family and loved ones. We can stop avoiding the unpleasant situations as we then know that the thoughts and emotions associated with these situations are not going to last long. They may even be significant life-lessons in hiding, which we're progressively more ready, willing and able to deal with more positively through the steps of working with the mind we've covered to this point. To be aware of, pay attention to and allow whatever our experience is, to not avoid it, to accept it and not deny it as the present moment experience, not to wish it to be other-wise, to acknowledge our (and other's) inherent reaction to what occurs, then to advance our understanding and experience to appreciate this process and transform our outlook and current state of mind on what our present life situation may be – this is working with the mind!

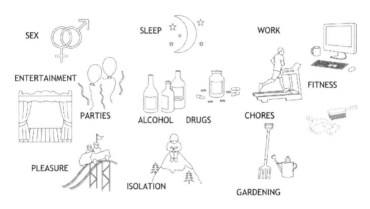

Figure 5.0 Positive engagement, or escapism?

Some common avoidance habits are shown in **Figure 5.0**, as all activities can be engaged in wholesomely or in the spirit of escapism and disassociation. We routinely use sensation (e.g. sex, entertainment, parties and pleasure), numbness (e.g. sleep, isolation, or intoxication), or activity (such as exercise, work or duties) to stay distracted. There's nothing wrong with hard work, diligence to duty or having fun, but in observing a continuous cycle of these routines we leave no time for deliberately address-ing our minds and our core values of the self. Because of this we seldom observe ourselves and the roots of poor states of mind that get cultivated in the subconscious, until they pop into the foreground of the conscious mind as they occasionally do[12] and catch our attention. As we notice some time spent abstaining from these activities and engaged in specific practice of working with the mind we see the extent to which the mind clings to the states induced through continued self-distraction, and the effects these have on ourselves and the family. The consequences of our states of mind, and habitual ways of reacting to people and situations often comes as a surprise to many of us. When we do not take time to carefully seek within, we risk remaining where we are in life, never developing new abilities to handle new conflicts and challenges that life brings. We don't live our lives fully, and can end up becoming stagnant.

We cannot stop certain negative events from occurring in our lives, but we can train our minds to stop reacting to these pains and suffering in ways that further contribute to frustration, or otherwise poor states of mind. We can be compassionate towards ourselves at these moments of vulnerability, accepting them with gratitude and letting go of the urge to avoid, or do something about any feelings that arise and any judgements we have about ourselves and others. Once we start avoiding the avoidance, if you will, and just appreciate what comes our way in life, difficulties may start feeling more brief, the thoughts and frames of mind which we are caught up in and further contribute to challenging states of mind diminish – and both can begin to seem an interesting and necessary part of life.

How can practicing awareness and attention lead us from allowing what's there and *acccpting* what arises to actually *appreciating* what arises? This means entering the realms of genuinely working with our minds and the contents of our day-to-day cognitive processes, from thinking and reflecting, to *feeling* something different, more empowering and positive, compared to how we have previously dealt with life events. Being grateful for what's there, is symptomatic of our practice advancing beyond merely playing with attention, to a place where we begin to experience how this practice is benefiting us. This can be very subtle to begin with, depending on our habits, characteristics and individual lifestyles and family situations. Why else do we really do anything in life, other than because we get something out of it that makes the doing worthwhile?

Perhaps it is subtle to begin with, but we may begin to recognise that we are calmer, or more able to return to balance after turmoil, emotion, stress or other difficulty. We may realise our interactions within the family are more tempered and controlled. To start with it's easy to appreciate some of the more obvious benefits, such as getting the time to ourselves to practise calm and relaxed feelings, lowered blood pressure[13], reduced stress[14], anxiety[15] and depressive symptoms[16], or any other of the positive effects from working with the mind.

So how do we go about appreciating the difficult things that we notice about ourselves? It's less easy to feel grateful for the pain, discomfort, loss and challenges we face but, again, with time and practice our brains begin to find it more straightforward to have a progressively growing resilience to such things quite naturally – almost as if an unintended by-product of doing the exercises. This can be thought of as like doing a physical set of exercises, with the intention to lose weight, for example. However, we also get fitter, stronger, and more flexible, and enjoy more energy and confidence when we exercise regularly or routinely, even if we didn't particularly have these goals in mind to start with. In much the same way, exercising our attention and awareness and following the steps of Working With The Mind means that when we have awareness of some negative aspect of present-moment life, we still see it as present-moment life. Just another issue arising that will fall away again soon, out of awareness. We don't treat it with further disdain or frustration, and we come to see the transitory, or changeable nature of all things – including even that which we experience as overwhelming. These are still just elements of our experience in life, and not the whole experience of life, or life itself. Many life lessons and learning points are easily and often overlooked because we see from our perspective only. Without working with the mind our autopilot state isn't particularly geared towards recognising that which isn't us or our idea of ourselves, unless it's affecting us, and we often only take note of this if consciously aware that it's affecting us negatively. The mind does this quite naturally and inherently as the brain processes information about the world around us in reference to ourselves (which we looked at in Chapter 1 under self-referential processing). Physically, our simple day-to-day ailments heal quite well by themselves generally, as long as some basic conditions are met and we have enough food and rest, for example. We may need more than mere time for our psychological ailments to heal however. Thinking about addictive tendencies, negativity, emotion, the mental aspects of health, and in dealing with our daily frames of mind and habits that have become negative and a hindrance, we can consider these issues as much a matter of opportunity as they are of time.

Left to its own devices, our mind can just as easily exacerbate problems as it can heal them, or grow from them; and there has to be some intervention to change perspective and make use of the opportunity to look beyond the immediate state of mind. Every moment in life represents an opportunity for this intervention, however our state of mind at that given moment may prohibit us from making the most of it. Appreciation is the first part of a key focus on the positive and deliberately paying attention in a constructive frame of mind, so as to enable us to seize on the opportunity for development. This can flip the unfortunately ingrained perspective of entitlement to life, where the basic needs we have as a guarantee which are taken for granted, can be turned into the opportunity to notice and reflect on how fortunate we are.

This is true because despite all the difficulties we face, our challenges in life are rarely connected to the basic needs of life, (which we discuss further in Chapter 8). There are many subtleties, layers or levels of difficulties and 'being stuck' which we notice by making this change in our perspective. If this may seem a strange thing to describe this way, let's take the example of a banana: if we have never had the experience or any understanding of a banana, someone uses words and their understanding and experience to describe it to us. They may say 'fruit', then describe its colour, how it grows, what it looks and tastes like, for example. In this way we begin to gain our own understanding of bananas, and we can have our own experience of this simply by trying a banana, and this supplements any understanding gained. In the same way, as we try these exercises for ourselves and build on our experience and understanding, the ability to view challenges from an altered perspective becomes more straightforward.

People from all walks of life experience traumas, negative experiences, collections of past events, memories, future projections of fears, and general difficulties in life that can present themselves within any space of the mind. 'Right' effort is certainly key when considering staying present with difficult experiences[17], and we must strike a personal and individual balance when opening up to what is present without seeking, striving or grasping at and empowering any state of mind that is present. After some practice with working with the mind it is essentially down to ourselves to explore this balance, and wavering one way or another is a natural part of the process of realising this balance for ourselves.

Delving further into difficulty when it arises, or away from dealing with it when it is present and too overwhelming, is easier with the help of a facilitator to guide this process, but they cannot do the balancing for us and our own understanding and experience is key. A negative experience can cause very profound challenges and it is not easy being present with these because some aspects of family, our mental self and life experiences are not easy to deal with or to accept. Quite often some of these aspects are painful to even give a small amount of attention to, and in this manner developing a positive, constructive strength to our cognitive process is immensely beneficial in life. Through greater appreciation we can realise the sheer number of opportunities for us to engage with such developing, healing and growing of our mind each day, and the effects this has on family life as well as life in general.

In the next chapter we will introduce some exercises for looking more specifically at our thoughts, and starting to look at what is difficult in our present experience of family life. There's no need to expect all challenges to disappear from our current family experiences, because these can be viewed as opportunities for family growth, nor to fear difficult or traumatic thoughts because these are just thoughts (something that we'll dive deeper into soon). In working with the mind an understanding and experience of finding a balance between them, helps us to identify the means by which we can genuinely remove much of what's difficult about the challenge faced, and look at difficult thoughts, experiences and events more openly. As we come to the last exercise chapter towards the end of the book, we focus in on identifying and transforming the more negative states of mind we have, but let's first look at some practices for being able to be present with our thoughts without being overwhelmed.

Obstacles to establishing practice

All difficulties faced stem from an
impercipience of self.

This conditions our expectations of what should
and should not happen to us in life.

*W*hy is it that we often don't seem to get the best of situations in life, and things don't go our way? Even when we try something new and positive it often ends all too quickly, and motivation runs out as we still have to deal with family, friends, work and life on top of this new resolution for change. Adapting the exercises introduced in the book is important, and will become easier and more naturally familiar. We become more attuned to mindfulness itself, and for this reason alone perhaps, it can be uncomfortable seeing what we start noticing. As we do there is often the thinking that we should be doing anything other than being still, wasting time. The autopilot mind-set and way of being is powerfully ingrained and conditioned in us. It is so easy to be entirely outwardly looking, and never inwardly seeing, such that allowing even a short time for introspection evolves into something quite helpful and transformative. A frame of mind arises that is progressively easier to call upon, offering the opportunity to redirect our attention when we notice the onset of negative or overwhelming frames of mind. Mindful family skills help so many areas of life, from being more aware of our parents, partners and children to managing matters when these relationships are difficult, damaging or in need of some more subtle attention. Essentially, this comes down to awareness and motivation which we cover in more depth in Chapter 8, but before we launch into the next set of practices it's helpful to consider briefly what obstacles to these we may have. This is to ensure some way of making sure the outcomes are as powerful, productive and positive as possible. Common obstacles to the benefits of mindfulness-based practices cause us to not do them, or to end up doing them with a focus that is expectant, distracted and without a real understanding or experience of the purpose and usefulness of the exercises[1].

To help us identify this for ourselves, we will soon come to specific obstacles after some practice. We'll do anything to avoid not doing anything, because when we do and we observe this, we see the awesome, vast, scary, intangible and ephemeral nature of everything in the mind. It is a paradox and a conundrum to want to see ourselves more clearly, but as we learn to just see and not to want to react as much to what we see, we glimpse this clarity. It's advised that we watch carefully as we settle into the practice of working with the mind and become more familiar with these patterns[2] of obstacles because our state of mind is so effective at swaying our decisions away from something unfamiliar. We may end up convincing ourselves not to do these practices, or to only do them with a half-hearted focus. As we'll see in Chapter 8, the frame of mind with which we approach our training can be almost as significant as the practice itself, and paying attention to this is certainly the way to stop the mind from finding reasons not to practice.

Moving with Awareness

Movement is a common anchor because it is easy to facilitate a heightened awareness of this into daily life and the practice can feel less like formally practicing or meditating, throwing up fewer barriers and reasons in the mind for not doing it. It may also be quite complex for some of us to notice breathing sensations, and it's not unusual to have initial difficulty connecting with some practices built on this idea. Moving can be an effective way of refocusing the attention to a set point after we're aware it has wandered. A repetitive movement pattern works well in this regard, as we breathe in sync with the pattern of movement; it can be more straightforward to get into the flow of following this type of pattern with the attention. All practices will have some benefits, but it is important, and perhaps more so for today's busy life-style, for us to enjoy or experience some ease of practice (especially for those of us just beginning). Further programme structures and guided exercises to follow and adapt can be found at the end of the book, in **Appendices 1 and 4**. These will guide the process of working with the mind and help support our understanding and experience to a point where we can learn what seems to work best for us.

Movement is an important part of this programme, and almost always a helpful practice because we can adapt the **Moving with Awareness** exercise to fit any of life's activities that involve movement. Steps to follow during this exercise are laid out below, but remember to make use of the guided audios that are available. Spend some time on each of the steps below, until you feel more comfortable and familiar with them so you can extend this gradually and practise without the audio. Read through the steps first, perhaps, to gain an understanding of what the practice involves, then follow the guided audio practice without the book. First find somewhere to walk up and down, preferably somewhere you won't feel concerned about on-lookers or getting in anyone's way. This can be inside or outside, and the length of the 'walk' need only be a few paces if practising in a confined space.

- Standing at one end of the walk, keeping the feet parallel to each other and shoulder-width apart, with the knees gently flexed and not locked. Allowing the arms to hang gently by the side of the body, or holding the hands loosely together in front of the body. Connecting with the breath, and perhaps briefly scanning the body, noting any sensations before directing the gaze softly ahead; slightly lowered and still aware of everything in the periphery of vision.

- Bringing the focus of awareness to the bottoms of the feet, getting a direct sense of the physical sensations of the contact of the feet with the ground, and the weight of the body transmitted through the legs and feet out into the ground. Perhaps flexing the knees slightly a few times to get a clearer sense of the sensations in the feet and legs and notice the balance of the body

- When it feels comfortable, transferring the major part of the weight of the body into the right leg, noticing the changing pattern of physical sensations in the legs and feet, as the left leg no longer bears as much weight.

- Allowing the left heel to rise slowly from the floor, noticing all the subtle movements involved, the sensations in the calf muscles, as the left foot lifts gently until only the toes are in contact with the floor. Aware of the physical sensations in the feet and legs, slowly lift the left foot, carefully moving it forward and feeling the foot and leg as they move through the air, then placing the heel out in front on the floor. Allowing the rest of the bottom of the left foot to make contact with the floor, transferring the weight of the body into the left leg and foot, aware of the sensations in the right leg as the right heel leaves the floor.

- With the weight fully transferred to the left leg, allowing the rest of the right foot to lift and move slowly forward, aware of the changing patterns of physical sensations in the foot and leg. Focusing attention on the right heel as it makes contact with the ground, transferring the weight of the body into the right foot as it is placed gently ahead, aware of the shifting pattern of physical sensations in the two legs and feet.

- Walking at a pace that is slower than usual, allowing the opportunity to be fully aware of the movements involved in the walking. In this way slowly moving from one end of the walk to the other. Aware particularly of the sensations in the bottoms of the feet and heels, as they make contact with the floor and of the sensations in the muscles of the legs, as they swing forward. Perhaps aware of the cycle of breathing in sync with the patterns of movement involved in the walking process

- At the end of the walk, stop for a few moments, then turn slowly around, aware of and appreciating the complex pattern of movements through which the body changes direction, and continues walking.

- Walking up and down in this way, being aware as much as possible, of physical sensations in the feet and legs, and of the contact of the feet with the floor.

Keeping the gaze directed softly ahead and lowered slightly.

- When noticing that the mind has wandered away from awareness of the sensations of walking, gently escorting the focus of attention back to the sensations in the feet and legs noticing the subtle interplay of muscle and movement balancing the body.

- In your own time bringing the walk to a natural end, taking a few moments at the end of the walk to release any awareness from this practice.

Start this practice for 5 -10 minutes, or longer, if it is comfortable. Really slow down the movements, as far as it's possible to do so (balance can get interesting, as you'll see), to guide the mind to tune in to the subtle changes in sensation as the body moves. It may be worth experimenting through this exercise as well, by walking at faster speeds, up to and beyond normal walking speed. When feeling particularly agitated, it may be helpful to begin walking quickly with awareness, and to slow down naturally as this state of mind settles. As often as is comfortable, bring the same kind of awareness cultivated in walking meditation to normal, everyday experiences of walking. As we come to a longer practice, and as we attend any prolonged period of focus in mindful exercises, movement practices break up other stages of awareness nicely. Mindfulness of movement is easily adapted to daily routines through sports or activities which we regularly observe. For further guidance on this, refer to **Appendix 1) Further support** which details other guided practices freely available through the online community group.

Mindful of Thoughts

Noticing thoughts can be an interesting experience. Actually, much of our thought process is fairly random and appears meaningless; it's the mind filtering through information which it has perceived before, or projecting and imagining what's to come. There is much interest in understanding the origin of thought, and it's suggested there is an automatic and a more reasoning, conscious system of thinking in the mind[3]. When subjected to some deliberate mindful awareness, the stream of thoughts can be quite intriguing to watch, because most of the time we do not allow a conscious, clear observation of the process of thoughts rising up and falling away from the mind. The thinking process that takes place in the background runs entirely automatically and habitually and we usually only have awareness of it when it starts to trouble or excite us. When thoughts become worth noticing, it's usually because they trigger a reaction or we may be inclined to reflect upon what arose in our thinking at that particular point. We're very closely attached to our own sense of rifling through our thoughts, and are too close to our own opinions that arise out of them or in response to this thinking, to be objective and open about it. We take thought for automatic fact, truth or something that we must cling to because it came from within us, are about what happened to us, so they appear to be true to us. As we observe the mind thinking and allow it some space to meander through thought, we quickly see how many thoughts are in the mind. In the **Mindful of Thoughts** practice we notice how largely uncontrolled thoughts are, how frequent or inappropriate they can be, and just how unintelligible they may be at their root.

The thoughts are unfiltered, and in accepting that they're not formed of anything other than replaying information in the mind, can be quite relieving to those of us who have recognised that the stream of thoughts contains things we don't necessarily like, approve of or find particularly beneficial to our experience of life. This exercise guides us to observe our thoughts, and what we think about them, through a more open perspective and without getting caught up in the stream of thoughts. This is built on in later practices, to include a focus on conscious and deliberate thought, but for now we are just observing what passes through the mind by itself; noticing how we are inclined to react to it. There are other practices for establishing mindfulness of thoughts, that are available through the WWTM community, and steps to follow during the **Mindful of Thoughts** exercise are laid out below. Again, make use of the guided audio that is available until more confident to extend this gradually and practise without it. Read through the steps first to gain an understanding of the practice, then follow the guided audio practice without the book.

- Beginning with some awareness of the breath, and allowing the body to settle into a comfortable position to practise in, take a few moments to connect the attention onto the breath

- Noticing where the breath cycle is clearest for you, just as it occurs naturally in this space, without feeling the need to alter the ryhthm or pace, just noticing the inbreath, where in the body is it most easily sensed. Then the outbreath, and where the sensations of breathing are most notable. Perhaps with a hand on the chest or lower abdomen to help identify these sensations.

- When it feels comfortable, lowering the gaze or clos-ing the eyes, focusing on the cycle of the breath into, and out of the body; aware of the sensations of the breathing for a few moments.

- Whilst breathing normally, noticing the stream of thoughts in the mind's eye, so that the objects of awareness are now thoughts in the mind, still notic-ing the gentle pace of the breath as we establish this awareness.

- As if listening to sounds, focusing the attention on whatever thoughts arise, noticing them start, develop, and pass away, holding in awareness the stream of thoughts arising in the mind in this moment.

- Thoughts come and go without conscious effort all throughout life, whilst breathing now consciously noting when thoughts arise, focusing attention on them as they pass through the space of the mind and eventually disappear.

- There is no need to focus on specific thoughts, or try to make thoughts come or go. Just allowing them to arise naturally.

- Does the stream of thoughts contain anything expected, or any surprises? Perhaps related to the days events, or recent happenings; observing the feel or content of each thought, maybe unrelated and wandering.

- Just aware of whatever thoughts are present, as they come into the mind. Not reacting to any of them, just observing, as if from outside the mind seeing what passes in and out of it.

- Realising when the mind is distracted by something else, or when it lingers on a particular thought, perhaps adding further to the story and chain of thinking as it arises, gently bringing the mind back to paying attention in the present moment and the breath; noticing the entire thought stream and all its contents coming and going, aware and letting go of attention of the distraction or lingering thought.

- Noticing the "quality" of the thoughts that arise, are they pleasant? Distasteful? Judging? Emotionally charged? Frustrated? Bored? Focusing on the conscious thought "whatever thoughts are present are neither right nor wrong, good nor bad; they're just part of this moment as it arises".

- If any thoughts bring with them intense feelings or emotions, pleasant or unpleasant, as best we can, noting their "emotional charge" and intensity, then letting them be as they already are.

- Noticing any of this going on where intense feelings arise. Then seeing if it is possible to focus again on the breath and a sense of the body as a whole, sitting and breathing, using this focus to anchor and stabilize the awareness for particularly emotion-driving thoughts.

- Releasing the awareness of the stream of thoughts, and focusing for a few minutes of the cycles of the breath entering and leaving the body. When it feels comfortable, bringing the practice to an end, perhaps resting a moment in the space of awareness before opening the eyes or raising the gaze.

The first thing that may be noticed once we have done this exercise a few times, is that the contents of the mind are hugely changeable and sometimes in this practice the mind is incessantly busy, continuously chattering away. It may be seemingly impossible to notice one thought ending and the next beginning, and yet at other times it's still and empty, as if devoid of all thought. With only a little understanding and experience we can appreciate that the contents of our thoughts are by no means permanent[4], and yet they frequently seem to trouble us. Our thoughts are often closely linked to our experiences, emotions and memories, all of which influence habitual reaction and instinctive decision-making. Similar decision-making habits have been noted in those who had professional experiences in common, such as jobs and skills that require acting under pressure, as discussed by Malcolm Gladwell[5] concerning the exchanges between traders and generals, for example.

Experience and memory can, in turn, affect the emotional states and frames of mind we experience (see **Figure 6.0**). The pattern of emotional arousal in us becomes repetitive and cyclical as our thoughts trigger further thoughts, and memories or experiences arise. The combined feeling is self-fulfilling then. We subconsciously find a reason to conform to the emotional state that builds after an event or an experience. How we feel is justified in the mind, regardless of the fact that the experience or event itself cannot be the sole factor contributing to our feelings as we discussed in **Figure 3.1**). We are free to choose our own thoughts, to influence our own states and do not have to believe everything that we think[6]!

Using specific and deliberate thoughts during practice is something we build up to in the next exercise chapter, and this can be helpful in framing our inner dialogue as part of a change to a more positive focus (as we'll discuss in the coming chapters). Overwhelming and negative states of mind have a lot of their roots in our subconscious thought processes and, therefore, doing the **Mindful of Thoughts** exercise regularly helps us to see thoughts in conscious awareness. With practice and greater awareness of thoughts we have more options for transforming our most inhibiting states which impact on us and our family most negatively. The mind processing sensations, thoughts and emotions can be likened to a drop in a pond — thoughts generate further thoughts, as ripples in a pond generate more ripples. Unless we use an awareness of this to direct our attention, by establishing the skill of being a bit more mindful, we very easily become lost in thought by thinking!

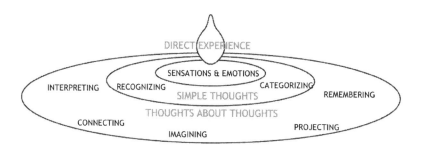

Figure 6.0: Ripples of thought

Working with the mind helps us to notice the cycle of thoughts, and a mindful state of mind enables us to consciously switch the focus of our attention while we are lost in our thoughts, which helps us to avoid the continued strengthening and expression of emotional states and reactions based on them. These emotions and reactions are often the reasons behind failed relationships, ill health and our generally unhelpful approaches to family life and well-being. As we continually break this cycle our reactions, thoughts and emotions become more controllable and changeable; and we have more fulfilling relationships, a sense of well-being and alleviation of pain or other discomfort from our life. We will develop the idea of using other senses to switch focus from thoughts as they become overwhelming, and when we get 'lost' in the chain of thought.

Thoughts are cyclical by nature, and much of the inherent difficulties we have in dealing with challenging thoughts, and the results they have in our lives, come from the way we ruminate over these[7]. But remember that whilst working through these practices there is no need to spend all day trying to be aware of thoughts! Remember balance so that clearer understanding and experience of the mind is of benefit to the self and others. The concern over available time to work with the mind need not be a hindrance to practice, because practising these skills in 'real life' within the family has a far greater immediate positive potential for our family and others. Finding ways to make our daily routine mindful[8], and including some self-compassion[9] (see Chapter 9) are both good places to start when considering fitting mindfulness into the hectic life of family!

Obstacles to practice can be *energetic*, either as slothful or agitated states where we're unable to be present and focused because of tiredness and a lack of energy, or because of hyperactivity and excessive energy. *Desire* can be an obstacle as well, because we notice ourselves wanting something, or wanting to be rid of something quite often when attempting to establish mindful states. We get distracted by thoughts of and urges to alleviate rising discomfort, of going to do something more pleasurable, of remembering situations that were pleasing and enjoyable and the mind then reflects on that which sparks our desire for gratification. It may become easier to sit in such a state of distraction or disassociation for longer, but this is not the fullest extent of practice.

Difficulty arises in the form of challenging, traumatic or annoying and uncomfortable memories, perhaps pain and discomfort in the body, thoughts of situations, aspects of our lives, and of people who have annoyed us and things that illicit in us a strong desire not to have them in our experience of life. Disturbing inner thoughts and questions while we're trying to settle more deeply mentally, is an obstacle of *doubt*, when our resolve in our own understanding and experience is shaken and tested during practice. These obstacles (energy, desire and doubt) are lessons learned through continued self-development, and it can be difficult to relate the value and learning of these because they must be understood and experienced for ourselves. We have actually already looked at the root-cause of obstacles in Chapters 1 and 4, when we looked at sensory gating and the mind's tendency to focus in quite naturally on the negative or difficult, respectively.

Even when we intend a positive change, this is often through a frame of mind governed by a negative focus. Guarding the sensory doors, meaning being aware when what we sense and perceive is giving rise to harmful states of mind and body, helps us understand and experience more openly that obstacles arise naturally and repetitively. For example, through the **Mindful of Thoughts** exercise we can come to notice our thoughts during the day more easily, and interrupt the autopilot thinking that can contribute to the difficulties we experience. If positive interactions and family plans can be made in thought, they can also be sabotaged and undone in thought too! In this sense, by staying present and paying attention to suitable anchors we can work to avoid hindrances, and do something about them when they arise. This process grounds us when the challenges of everyday and family life would usually push us into reacting negatively. The best way of working with an obstacle once we recognise it, is to avoid thinking, experiences, over-indulgence and sensations that lead to non-productive states of energy, desire or doubt, preventing them from arising where we can. We also have the option to transform our states of energy, desire and doubt as they arise and become a hindrance, through a different, positive anchor for our attention, creating a new state (as we'll focus on in the remaining chapters).

A thorough understanding of the experience of mindfulness-based practice within scientific realms is growing, as we delve more and more into research around this process of working with the mind. Although still in its infancy compared to larger mainstream health research such as heart disease for instance, (which had 20 times more research papers published compared to mindfulness in 2016), the benefits of mindfulness-based practices and programmes are subject to a growing prevalence of studies. There's an exponential increase in numbers of papers published since 2000, although a gap in practical understanding and experience of using mindfulness-based exercises, tools and practices nevertheless still exists, even though many have heard of it. It can still be a concept that may often evoke much resistance or mixed response, perhaps because it ostensibly goes against a natural flow of things. We don't take the necessary time to be still, and it feels unusual or uncomfortable to do so. Being open with ourselves, or our development as individuals isn't common and is sometimes quite difficult to do. Even within our families, observing such open, honest and vulnerable interaction isn't the norm because we want to shelter our loved ones from our weaknesses and avoid having to deal with the challenge of being affected by theirs.

Many of the programmes, courses and much of the

support accessible to help us do this are easily ignored, often largely because they're not tailored to our specific needs or interest and so the benefit is overlooked. What's right for some certainly isn't for others, and families are no exception to this rule. As we start to notice our individual barriers and boundaries, and those of the rest of the family, we can also notice our reactions to the practices we have covered and those we'll come to. This can be a useful tool and we don't actually have to 'do well' at working with the mind for it to work. The natural changes that arise through the exercises involved allow us to see ourselves in an ever-expanding light which helps to undo some of the conditioned ways that we expect things to go in life. As we progressively strengthen and reinforce a mindful space of awareness, from which bearing witness openly and non-reactively is possible, we see that we don't really succeed or fail in these exercises – merely develop! When we're overwhelmed, it is easier to gradually come back to a calm space, knowing that even through our most positive intentions and open awareness we still lack the foresight enough to understand our needs and our future beyond our current state of self and experience. Knowing that difficulties we face are of the self (or self-referential states of mind and perspectives), we can expand our minds, and seeing ourselves more objectively becomes less overwhelming, even in difficulty.

Another aspect of ourselves which is beneficial to family, and which develops through this practice is our kind and loving nature. This is perhaps a little more subtle than being aware and paying some attention to difficulty. Like appreciation, it grows of its own accord as we adapt working with the mind to our needs and lifestyles. Clearly kindness and love are key to family and our relationships and interactions with each other. So, if we don't continually have a greater love and kindness in our outlook for both ourselves and our family, ultimately we do both a disservice. However, how do we actively cultivate these aspects of character? This is what we'll be looking at in the next chapter.

Affection

We experience ourself, our thoughts and feelings as something separated from the rest, a kind of optical delusion of consciousness.

This delusion is a kind of prison for us, restricting us to our personal desires and to affection for a few persons nearest to us.

Our task must be to free ourselves from this prison by widening our circle of compassion to embrace all living creatures and the whole of nature in it's beauty.

*I*f we don't have powerful or positive feelings about ourselves or our family, we're all the more easily overwhelmed individually and collectively as a family when there are negative experiences and feelings present. One of the most important things we can do as people is to develop this positive quality; this important foundation is fundamentally about love, and a progressive ability to be able to think, speak and act in such terms. We are quite naturally distanced from the idea of love, for ourselves or others, and an interpretation of love is actually quite complicated; because our perspective on it can alter love into becoming something other than what it actually is at its core. It is quite common to consider a focus on love as weakness, as being soft or even as something that's not really accessible or acceptable to us. Attachment isn't love, and expecting happiness out of our interactions and associations with family can cause pain in the event of difficulty and challenge, which are a natural part of family life. Any kind of relationship where we imagine we can fulfil ourselves through others will cause pain, because it is not in our family's duty or power to make us happy, nor in ours to do so for them. Fulfilment and contentment in our self allows us to nurture and appreciate that in another, but expecting fulfilment from another is a sure path to a destructive relationship and family unit.

We tend to find kindness, compassion and love (or what we'll refer to collectively as affection for simplicity's sake) restricted in life. Just as it is simpler for us to become wrapped up in, and focused on our own individual desires in preference over other people's, so too is it more straightforward for us to limit our affection to being only for those nearest and dearest to us (whether this is conscious and deliberate or not), as opposed to extending affection to those less familiar to us[1]. This is due to the fact that we process information from the world around us through only our own narrow perspective, forgetting that this is just one individual's way of seeing the world. It's very easy in this natural automatic state of narrow or self-focus, to overlook some of the suffering or difficulties of others which is inherent in the world more broadly. Our lives are more intertwined individually and collectively today than ever before in history because we are interdependent for resources, technology, information and communication, among many other important life essentials. Yet we are less evolved in our mind-set than we could be, considering how interconnected we are. Arguably very little of our attention and energy is spent on our individual and collective psychological well-being, how our minds work and the impacts of this, compared to the scale of our awareness of the efforts and attention paid to the impacts of other human endeavours, such as our scientific and technological understandings, for example. We allow very little of our time to truly reflect on the nature of our interdependence, and the significance of our connectedness in the simplest aspects of daily life. We looked into this in Chapter 5 as a tool to change our state of mind away from an automatic inclination to focus on the negative in situations. Here we'll delve a little deeper into the value of extending our perspective beyond the individual self, and the implications that a focus on affection can have on the most devastating frames of mind and negative experiences that we can come to experience[2].

Using kindness and compassion as mindful tools helps considerably in re-wiring the familiar cognitive processes and habitual thinking patterns we tend to have. The value of affection which we can benefit hugely from on a personal level, is arguably also something that family and society is in great need of today. We live in a world of perceptual boundaries, where we view the world through a unique individual filter. Our minds are predominantly predisposed towards a less deliberately-conscious awareness of those with different boundaries, which leaves us more inclined towards judgement and negative habitual processes, such as bias, intolerance and resentment. Even where our normal thinking has become negative, we're still inclined to consider it to be rational[3]! More negative and destructive states of mind such as anger and hatred can easily grow out of this, and positive habits of thought and emotional states can become seemingly more difficult to instigate. The international significance of this is mirrored on smaller scales within the family, and we see that a true way forward for relating more constructively with each other is through working with the mind to address this psychological predisposition.

Kindness, compassion and love are actually quite straightforward to cultivate and like all exercises of the mind, have an immediately powerful impact on our daily lives, when we include them in our days and weeks through simple practices. There are numerous, remarkable stories of the immediate effects that affection can have when expressed toward those around us as well as upon ourselves[4]. Kindness can be a thought or an act of behaviour, typically expressed (by thinking or acting) in a way to alleviate our suffering and that of others. This can be a subtle thing to do and does not have to be a grand gesture. Acts of kindness that put the suffering of other people first, do not have to prove some point as we engage with them, nor do they have to provide some personal gratification or recognition of any sort. We may find it feels good to think and act kindly and this doesn't necessarily undermine the kindness itself, so long as the outcome arises from an intention to reduce suffering. Kindness is kindness even if there is some motive of personal gratification involved, and even where this affection is directed at ourselves and not others.

Compassion reflects the feeling or suffering of another and is the motivation behind an act of kindness. One of the attributes of people more commonly unique and fundamental to humanity is the ability to be compassionate beings. It begins with sympathy – feeling sorry for someone's misfortune and suffering, empathy – understanding the feelings and suffering of someone else, and compassion then takes on a concern for the suffering of someone. The Dalai Lama has been quoted describing compassion as "fostering genuine concern for others' difficulties and pain, and developing close, warm-hearted feelings for others. Not only for family and close friends, but for everyone, enemies too"[5]. The desire to alleviate this suffering, (our own or someone else's) is the compassion behind the act or thought of loving kindness. These are deliberate processes, which can be practised as we shall discuss in Chapter 9, and the state of mind governed by reflecting on affection is key for these practices to begin to bear fruit.

From conception, (when our being is conceived) to

parturition (when we are born) love is the driving force for that coming into being. This can be subtle to appreciate if, for example, there's no love specifically between our parents; nevertheless, the sheer miraculous nature of the coming together of all the people and situations that enabled our parents to conceive and give birth is itself of a greater force of love. Here the word love is used to describe the creative force of our genes, flowing from some ancestral source through us to some future generation, and the connection between our biological parents who were the link in this chain immediately prior to us. Whilst considering affection it's important to point out that actually love has many forms[6], and our ideas of love can be as equally misconstrued depending on our perspectives, opinions and states of mind on which they're predicated. From our individual perspective of love, we only see from our point of view that we love, and the subject of our love can become more subjective because we are the one doing the loving. In other words we again experience this as a self-referential process, more engaged with the focus on 'I' rather than the love or the subject of it. 'WIIFM', or 'what's in it for me?' is a constant default mode of the mind without our deliberate intervention – even in love. So as we love our family we do so from the self-experience, and this has only potential as limited as we ourselves and our habitual states of mind are. Regardless of our inclination for self-focus, or the form of love that we have in mind, we're better served thinking of love for family (and others actually) as the driving force behind the compassion we observe whilst working with our minds. This is a different perspective to the usual expectation that love should have to be self-centred, sought out to make us feel good and not be about a focus on making others feel good.

Too often is it assumed that kind and compassionate people are just so by nature, and conversely that unkind and uncaring people are so too; yet in reality these are both just outcomes of routine or habitual thinking, speaking and acting. This arises out of states of familiarity that are learned throughout life. Highly competitive learning and work environments and stressful family relationships can make us believe that the road to a successful career, or happy family life is through constantly pushing ourselves to extremes of our abilities and being hard on and self-critical of ourselves. Kindness and compassion, if considered at all, are often viewed as weaknesses and being soft-hearted as possibly leading to us to be unsuccessful in life or taken advantage of. However, the reality is quite different. Being judgemental and criticising ourselves and others will often lead to persistent negative emotions, or a build-up of significant negative mental and physical tension, self-doubt and a disconnect with other people such that we start viewing them from a space of being judgemental or emotionally affected. We have doubts about other people's intention, we don't trust people and are quick to anger or be frustrated about other's behaviour – something outside of our control.

Think for a while, what the world would look like if we could silence these cycling thoughts, this inner voice for a moment, and be more affectionate towards ourselves and others. A gentle, non-judgemental awareness of the present is certainly not an easy thing to develop in a short space of time, or from a long-developed and ingrained state of persistent negativity (usually from significant life challenges). The value of cultivating this outlook, however, is that it cannot be overcome by whatever negativity we have, because there is always the option of implementing some practice to 'come back to' a state of mindful awareness (and to establish this proactively too). For example, within the family context there are many reactive and stressful situations that arise, such as when parenting young children and dealing with the inevitable challenging situations this involves. Or when supporting and guiding older children through the changes of growing up and dealing with more powerful emotions, and perhaps in more volatile family situations where the actions and decisions of those in our family really rock the foundations of the whole family unit. All these can be perfect examples of when to use this ability to return to a mindful state, or to benefit from approaching difficulty with a proactive awareness and some understanding that we can't control others, but we can control how we feel in reaction to them and their actions.

Having a focus on affection within our family unit plays a vital role because of the natural challenges that arise over the duration of our family lives, including the difficulties of relating to each other and navigating through the inevitable dark times. Affection is an integral part of mindfully working with the mind and such a process is not undertaken in a truly open-minded manner until we embed the values of kindness and compassion within us and become more open-hearted. If opening our hearts on top of opening our minds sounds pretty far-fetched, it certainly isn't immediately or necessarily easy but it is simple and powerful! This is no mean feat, and for some (especially for those of us from a position or background of significant difficulty and challenge in life) this is quite an undertaking. However those of us this applies to also have the most to gain from a greater loving kindness, and the natural resilience it brings us. The natural flow of things is stacked against thinking affectionately, because we are inherently focused on just following our automatic ways of thinking. What is to be gained, is the undoing of this automatic state of mind and the results arising from it in life such as the current experiences and outcomes for family life where we prolong and exacerbate diffi-culty. We take away, or give out and cause, suffering from negative experiences, instead of letting them be difficult and focusing on what we can control in respect to them (ourselves). This process starts with ourselves, as with-out developing self-kindness and self-compassion, true compassion can be difficult to feel towards others, and manifesting kindness towards someone else is only ever strengthened through self-compassion.

This starts simply by thinking about ourselves as we would anyone else going through difficulty, through a more objective perspective[7] instead of being hard on our-selves. We start with ourselves during affection prac-tices, and move outwards towards others from there, as we will come to see in Chapter 9. While doing the exer-cises to follow this process, we are being aware of our thoughts and emotions and accepting them as they are. This acceptance has to be done in a kind and tender way without being harsh on ourselves in any way. Our minds are often clogged with feelings like anger, remorse, stress, and the more subtle energies and precursors to these states. Instead of controlling or blaming ourselves, we need to be kind to ourselves. This is such a powerful tool that it not only changes the way we see ourselves, but also changes our mind-set and the way we see the world around us. We may be surprised to realise that the feelings we have towards others does not depend on the other person or their behaviour – it is all in our mind, it is entirely our decision. A real conundrum strikes us when we truly realise this truth applies to the feelings we have towards ourselves too, the paradox that it's our choice at some fundamental level to feel bad about life, although we don't *consciously* want to feel bad! This is because we are controlled by our conditioned patterns and do not know how to break our limiting habits[8] and, initially, this can be hard to get our heads around.

There is something to be said for forgiveness and in learning to allow our mistakes and shortcomings as a person. This is an integral element in developing kindness and compassion towards ourselves despite our flaws – nobody's perfect, and if we wait for this to feel better about ourselves we will waste a lot of life! We bring our own suffering, and our own thoughts, feelings and emotions into being through how we continually react to life's situations and circumstances. Consciousness is an expenditure or, more appropriately, a transfer of energy, and our attention (the focus of our conscious energy) is bound much of the time in a negative space, such as when realising we are frustrated with family, ourselves and our reaction to family, or that we are discontented without an awareness as to why. As we practice mindfulness of mind further and include an anchor of attention on kindness and compassion this affection relaxes our mind, we see ourselves and others in a new light in which we are less judgemental[9]. Deliberate attention on something positive and outside of this familiar automatic focus is very powerful because of this reason, and working with the mind, even reading this book for example, opens the mind to holding our focus in a positive space. We face difficulties with patience and become less reactive. When our brains are cleared from the usual clutter, we gain wisdom and skills to face difficulties and resolve them more easily. Then, as we become kinder towards others, we become more tolerant of our own situations in life and this cycle reinforces itself with continued effort.

Compassion is a strong feeling through which we connect ourselves momentarily to the suffering of others and wish for alleviation of all suffering. Many problems in the world today, including thoughts and acts of cultural, racial and sexual discrimination, and all violence (including in the name of religion), can all be attributed to a lack of compassion towards ourselves and others. There is no established consensus as to why some people can empathise quite naturally while others cannot, but some work into the empathy behind compassion suggests that exposure to testosterone in the womb impacts empathy of the developing brain[10]. Compassion appears to be a most fundamental and beautiful feeling; one that anyone can have or develop, even though it may seem to be initially awkward to evoke, and although many of us appear unable to develop a tendency to be compassionate to ourselves and others. It can seem very difficult, in fact, to understand the pain of others, while we usually view our own suffering self-indulgently – without true intent towards growth and learning from it. We sometimes do not open-up to our own pain, and our mind has the tendency to register others' pain and difficulty as less important. We withdraw ourselves from our own suffering and that of others because we simply want to avoid the negative feelings it would generate when we engage with pain and suffering, and having to change the way we look at our suffering. When deliberately aware of something uncomfortable, it's easy to get rid of the discomfort – we just look away! The problem this poses is that the challenging nature of what's uncomfortable doesn't go, just our deliberate and conscious awareness of it. Try as we may to coast through life with fingers in our ears and with our eyes closed in this way, ignoring things that sound and look daunting, this is never a positive way forwards – simply a comfortable way of avoiding having to deal with what challenge we may learn and grow from engaging with. In so doing we miss out on a gift of opportunity to develop which will keep repeating and repeating in life's situations as our state of mind is stuck on the 'why does this always happen to me?' focus of the pity-party mentality, until we're ready and willing to engage, learn and grow. "See no evil, hear no evil, speak no evil" is a useful slogan which originally implied an intent not to dwell on negative or 'evil' thoughts, deeds or speech, but this is too easily imbued with an idea of maintaining complete ignorance of, or deliberately looking away from our inherent negative focus and not wanting to be involved[11]. In today's world this is a backwards approach to changing an incompetent state of mind because if we do not develop awareness first, any approach to change will still result in neither the capacity to acknowledge the negative of an untamed mind, nor the competency to remain consistent in transforming this negative.

Mindfulness allows us to open up to compassion. As we meditate and start living more of our lives in the present, we come closer to non-judgemental observation of suffering in our own lives as well as the suffering of others. This process then gives rise quite naturally to the possibility of compassion. The first step is empathy. The simplest way of referring to empathy is an "ability to share another's emotions, thoughts, or feelings"[12]. Empathy happens when we pause for a moment and take a look at someone else's life. We come close to their pain, we acknowledge the distress they are going through. When we start looking with empathy towards others, we become tolerant of them. We start seeing them as another human being who is also going through their own pain and sufferings. Even if the person's behaviour appears disagreeable to us and somehow irritates our sense of things or goes against our perspective, we can disconnect with their behaviour and connect with the suffering that may be the reason behind a person's behaviour and habits. Compassion goes one step further when we actually have the urge to take action to alleviate the suffering; we want to put ourselves in others' shoes, feel their pain, and a strong desire to take action. Recent research has examined the link between mindfulness and increases in empathy, showing positive change toward emotional support, stress and resilience[13], all of which are key to developing and maintaining the positive family dynamic! It helps us to build more meaningful and fulfilling relationships with others, then supports an out-look and state of mind that is less influenced by negativity from challenging aspects of relationships, and an ability to quickly return to a space of more balanced perspective after a period of being overwhelmed. Regular acts of kindness help to re-wire the connections in our minds, leading to changes in the way we perceive ourselves and others as we incorporate kindness and empathy in our lives.

The way we relate to others internally, within the private confines of the mind and our opinions of them, influences our behaviour towards them. If we hold a grudge towards others at any level, we are likely to express that feeling in some way towards that person. This is an automatic reaction and we may not even realise that we have these intentions in mind, and we tend to exhibit such behaviour often without even being aware of it. Our minds instinctively find faults, judge and criticise. Empathy, as we discussed, is the first step toward understanding the sufferings of others, and reversing this instinct. Once we have understood empathy and have come closer to an awareness of our suffering without attachment to it, allowing our suffering and that of others, the next step is towards developing compassion. As we move towards compassion, we start relating to suffering in the world, gradually acknowledging and not avoiding it. We may start with small acts of generosity, simply being friendly to others or forgive ourselves and others of wrong-doing or bad behaviour. Gradually strengthening the pattern of compassion in our minds weakens the habitual responses of relating to the world negatively. **Figure 7.0** shows some ideas of how to practically begin to step away from an automatic, un-affectionate state of mind towards engaging empa-thetic regions of the brain.

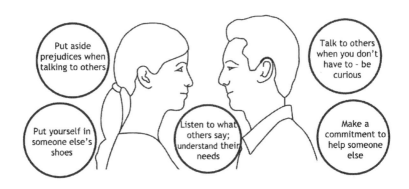

Figure 7.0 – Practically developing compassion

Soon enough a repetition of compassionate thoughts and practices allows us to forgive ourselves and others the perceived weaknesses and foibles we have – to err is human, after all. Extending this practice to others becomes a natural part of this process. We start under-standing that negative emotions are not a result of other's behaviour towards us, but rather the connections or pat-terns in our brains that trigger familiar reactions and emo-tions in response to perceived information and situations (in other words the brain constructs the emotions from our experience[14]). Mindful meditation can help to re-wire many of these connections, as we start observing more fulfilling and engaging ways of relating to ourselves and people around us (even in difficulty). In so doing, the emo-tion we construct can be less negative and overpowering.

By practising the exercises to develop kindness and compassion for some period of time, we will start observing subtle, positive changes. The first impact is on our inner thoughts, emotions and sensations, where we start intuitively believing in our capabilities rather than inherently doubting them, and become kinder towards our own 'weaknesses'. Our automatic patterns of reaction to others around us will change – whenever we are angry with someone, for example, we may usually simply avoid that person (or react to them). When practising mindful meditation, we start seeing that pattern clearly. Once we're familiar with this automatic, subconscious reaction we can begin to work consciously and in a more thought-out way. By using kindness and compassion as an anchor for affection, we can notice first how it feels to be angry with this person, in this example. What can we observe that contributes to this feeling of being angry, so that if we had to, how would we explain why we feel how we feel? This can be quite challenging actually, looking at emotion-ally-charged thought, sensation and speech. However, it is something that our practice of kindness and compassion can help to address as we cultivate an attitude of open, unconditional love, friendliness and generosity. For those of us naturally disinterested in such states, these prac-tices are still a powerful and practical tool for overcom-ing much of the difficulties of challenging relationships, emotions, and ways of relating to ourselves in life, and don't have to be thought of as somehow diminishing our strength of character. In fact, we find that they strengthen us progressively, and as difficulty arises within the family unit, we have a tool immediately available to help.

Practising mindfulness with kindness and compassion will have another major benefit. It helps us to recognise the fundamental connection among all human beings which is very useful when family life is getting hard! We have all experienced our own individual set of beliefs and struggles in this world, and are all in this experience of inter-connected life together. When we spend time aware that we are aware beings, we see this centre of awareness as the seat of the self[15], then, as this further increases the compassion we can have for ourselves and others, we become better human beings. Ultimately everyone suffers and desires some form of happiness, and although we can't change our struggles in life, and sometimes can't avoid getting into these difficult situations, we can control how we respond to these struggles and difficulties. Through working with the mind we can undo some of the 'wirings' in the mind which lead to limiting cycles of thoughts and responses, and instead, practice patterns of a more constructive nature.

As we'll come to understand and experience for ourselves, kindness and compassion are fundamental to this process, and are vastly underrated as virtues and qualities to instil in ourselves. Although there is always a spectrum, and we can strike a balance to find some happy medium, the absence of affection is devastating at individual, family and community levels.

Recent research measuring oxytocin levels in new parents, then oxytocin and cortisol in their babies over the first 12 months of life, suggested that the deliberate choice to be affectionate is pretty key. Oxytocin is a hormone released in the pituitary gland during experiences of social connection and bonding; it's key in the birthing process as a stimulant of contractions during labour and to shrink the uterus after parturition (birth). It's also linked as being key to the bonding process of primary care-giver and infant, even in men as shown by studies in 2012, where dads played more closely and intimately with infants after being administered with oxytocin[16]. More recently still, studies of dozens of same-sex male parent couples fathering through surrogacy, found naturally occurring levels of oxytocin in the fathers, equal to that of biological mothers[17]. The choice to care for and be affectionate to babies who weren't biologically theirs, triggered the same levels of oxytocin in the body as in mothers who conceived, carried, gave birth and cared for their child. Affection and the choice of deliberate care is a vital human necessity, one that we often link only to the very young and which gradually tails off, or which we limit to those immediately important to us.

Affectionate intentions within the family need not mean we must be responsible for others all the time, as this is unhelpful where they aren't enabled to develop for themselves. So, as with all things working with the mind, balance is vital so we don't imbue others with a sense of entitlement or the expectation that their fulfilment comes from anywhere but within themselves. In these same studies, cortisol (a stress hormone) levels in babies were higher, and brain scans of the regions responsive to stress measured as less reactive to stressful situations in infants where parents were immediately and consistently responsive to babies' cries for attention. For infants who weren't immediately comforted, but who were consistently attended to and not entirely ignored, stress hormone levels were lower, and brain regions responding to stress were more active – perhaps indicating that it's important to allow the developing mind to encounter stress but also to experience loving kindness. Although this is a simplified understanding, it highlights the significance of choosing to develop positive intention quite clearly, something quite automatic and strong when it comes to loving our kids – but something that is nonetheless readily available throughout life. Dog-lovers experience surges of oxytocin during play and bonding with their dogs for example[18], and in other studies, meditators measured before and after a focus on altruism and appreciation were noted to experience significant increases in oxytocin by the end of the practice[19]. The severe examples of lacking affection, or extreme difficulty in avoiding negative outcomes from overpowering destructive emotions, are potent stimulants to reflect on whilst considering cultivating affection. Marvyn Iheanacho, is such an extreme example, of how important this practice is, where he beat Alex Malcolm, a five-year-old to death in a park in the UK after the child lost a shoe in November 2016[20]. Witnesses heard a child's fearful voice saying "sorry", loud banging and a man screaming about the loss of a shoe. We all get angry, and all experience powerful emotions, the antidote to which is simply to practice an opposite and powerful emotion.

Even the intention we anchor to in practices such as those in Chapter 9, is enough to stimulate some positivity and we do not need to expect to feel immediately overcome by peace, love and understanding. Such practice will expand over time and the effects amplify, while emotional resilience is something that can more easily be established through a practice of working with the mind. Even love and kindness that we do have in ourselves is often very limited, self-attached and rarely extended beyond this shallow pool of familiarity and ease of affection. Emotional resilience, or the 'emotional quotient' and thinking differently about what the value of intelligence is and how it should be used, is important for a fulfilling life today. An intelligence quotient (IQ) is a score derived from standardised tests to determine intelligence; emotional intelligence or the emotional quotient (EQ) is an ability to influence our own emotions (or those of others). What we hold in consciousness is vital to our immediate family, because this forms who we are and determines our perpetual states of mind – and this is a deliberate choice! It becomes increasingly clear through working with the mind that we decide where our attention goes, or at least, that we can continually interrupt an automatic state of mind once we have awareness of it – and choose where to place our focus. Holding a reverence for emotional intelligence in conscious awareness is a wisdom often overlooked, and in today's world we value some virtues which are perhaps less potent to family and individual happiness or success than we assume.

We all wish for achievement or competence in our field of endeavours, and great knowledge and intellect is heralded as a grand purpose and pinnacle in the education of our children. "Work hard in school, learn lots, gain intelligence, and contribute to the world by getting a good job" seems to be the thinking behind the schooling process. Iheanacho is one of the many extreme examples of severe emotional difficulties, sadly resulting in tragedy, but there are many highly-educated and intelligent people through-out our modern history who have contributed to far more atrocious things than the murder of one child in an act of rage. Intellect can be twisted and become wrapped up in self-fulfilling cycles of judging that which doesn't meet its convoluted standards. 'Reflections on the Holocaust' touched upon the idea that potential for extreme barbar-ity is a matter of people's conscious and unconscious[21] – a sobering thought that actually good 'intelligent' people have a responsibility of knowledge, for even they can eas-ily contribute to hatred and violence. If we use our head, but not our heart there will be something lacking at some point in our endeavours – in whatever field of focus we are in. The suggestion here is merely that a focus on affection is indeed fundamental, without this family wouldn't really be anything more precious than just people together and with it the possibilities for growth are endless. For exam-ple, it is not possible to shout at or argue with our family members, or even to be frustrated with ourselves, while just being in a space of awareness as we do during prac-tice of working with the mind. This space of awareness or just sitting in conscious awareness can be applied in ret-rospect to a situation where we have been shouting at, or are currently shouting at our family (or just frustrated with ourselves). It is easier to start this process with a review of a past situation, than to engage awareness immediately in the present moment whilst such a scenario unfolds. However both are equally practical and achievable with a little practice in establishing our understanding in our experience of such an awareness. It's been noted that the human brain isn't intrinsically that effective at reflecting on empathy on a large scale[22], and from our own life experiences we see how challenging it may be to think about the lives of others compassionately. A mindful state of awareness *is* affection, and from here, exerting a more loving focus becomes more and more empowering and valuable, further enabling us to free ourselves from the prison of our current perception and the delusions this gives rise to time and again.

It is indeed worth aiming to "widen our circle of compassion", to expand our consciousness beyond our current delusions, as noted by Einstein. However, all things of the mind can become increasingly convoluted because they can be explained and expressed in so many ways. Unique to working with the mind, it is our own understanding and experience that is important. To this end, whatever our goals in doing this, in the next chapter we delve into how to consider what we aspire to, and what inspiration and motivation we can seek for our own benefit from these practices.

Associating and aiming

It is not our purpose to become each other; it is to recognise each other, to learn to see the other and honour them for what they are.

*W*e will never grow as people if we do not aspire to anything outside of the current experience of life, seek inspiration from the world and motivate ourselves to something positive or some progression from the here and now. We risk forever succumbing to our current emotional states, usual frames of mind of dealing with everyday and family life and what arises, if we do not aim beyond our current understanding and experience in life. In today's world there's much poverty of ambition which can severely limit us individually and as families. Poverty of ambition is as equally severe as corruption, financial poverty, devastation and famine, except this poverty is of the mind, of our outlook and expectations on life. When we do not aspire to something, and this can be anything, the mind stagnates and we do not progress, develop, learn or grow. In fact there is much ongoing research around the concept of inactivity, whether mental or physical, and the devastating effects this has on the brain[1]. However, a path with no obstacles probably leads nowhere, and so looking at our ambition (or lack thereof) is also a valuable opportunity to take into account what we may need to go through in life to get where we want.

Our potential for positive change and development as families and as individuals, is limited when we do not grow, learn and stimulate body, brain and mind. Working with the mind helps us enormously here to see more intuitively what we can aspire towards in our current life situation. In fact, meditation practices may even increase our life expectancy[2]! Many of us experience feeling powerless or trapped in current relationships and family life, often because of the accumulative and continuous subconscious conditioning from the world around us, making us think that things should be better but it's beyond our grasp to achieve this for ourselves. Unless we are fortunate enough to have a family unit around us which supports our growth and development, so that we can look at ourselves and our environment mindfully with an open and expanded awareness, we are likely to form the similar restricted habits of opinion and belief that unfortunately have become commonplace today. Examples of these are the embedded beliefs we hold but don't necessarily have conscious awareness of, and those everyday patterns where suffering and harmful outcomes for family are replayed over and over. Belief without awareness can be very challenging and self-limiting, for example where we assume we don't have to work at things like love, happiness and respect, merely expecting them to be in our lives without first a little cultivating instead[3]! It is generally very life-limiting when we feel that nothing particularly matters, during states of indifference where we don't really know, care about or open up to anything that isn't already a part of our comfort zone of the familiar life experience. This is real suffering and the true experience of a poverty of ambition, where we don't know why or how we are pained, but notice the outcome of it. It's perfectly normal to feel trapped, or to wish for more time to focus on ourselves. Ironically though, if left to our own devices, time and energy are the things we often make the least productive use of. In much the same way, we are also largely unaware of our emotions and states of mind, until we find ourselves reacting negatively. This can be thought of as a snowball effect, because seemingly insignificant thoughts and feelings quickly spiral into quite challenging and dangerous perspectives without having a good awareness of ourselves with which to see this process[4] (which is a good ambition to have).

In this section of the book we will reflect on aiming for something quite a lot, but it's important to know that we don't actually have to know what we're aiming for specifically if we don't already have life goals in mind. The process of starting to work with the mind as a more regular part of life, to look at ourselves openly and to expand our attention and awareness, goes hand in hand with working on values and goals as stepping stones along this process of self-development. We will consider here the means of keeping ourselves constantly aspiring, inspired and motivated, because of the risks of becoming caught up in negative focus on improvement and a mind-set focused on striving. Remember Desiderate, and the line, "beyond a wholesome discipline be gentle with yourself"[5], because it is important while looking more intently at ourselves and our negative habits, to notice that time *off* from this is equally as important as time focused *on* it. True well-being is a balance in constant flux, and this is why a greater self-awareness has the fundamental potential to help us forever adapt to our changing needs because we are aware of this constant ebb and flow. We find that it is our desires that cause difficulty and suffering, and even where our needs aren't actually met, it is our desire that we are so troubled by. Needs are generally fulfilled as and when they should be, and as we pay attention with greater ability, we can see this for ourselves intuitively. However, because we're so caught up in desire, we notice that they are never fulfilled, as represented in **Figure 8.0** below.

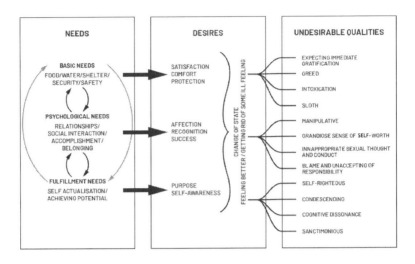

Figure 8.0 – Desiring a 'better' state often causes our undesirable qualities

Time to relax and be still is important, even if we are aiming for an improved ability to be energetic, focused and productive. As we look at our values and aim for change in aspects of life which are not how we wish them, this change is progressive; it is a gradual realisation of something to look towards that we find worthy. In this way, we learn and experience through small repetitions which accumulate towards some greater change over time. It is important, therefore, to allow ourselves the space to be gentle with ourselves whilst observing this wholesome discipline (not being too extreme or strict). Because time is involved we must remember not to expect immediate drastic change and thereby lead ourselves to further neg-ativity, sabotaging our positive intent. We have to notice that when we need time just to be ourselves, to stop and to be as we are even if at that moment is not necessarily where or what we want to be. This is an important balance to be able to be aware of, and to find and realise for ourselves. That is not to say that we stop everything that we are trying to change for the positive completely and forever. It is to notice when that aim has become a negative focus, or is starting to make us feel tired, burnt out or less positive in our motivation to work towards this goal. Giving ourselves the time to form some intent to feel good again is key, even if that is to engage or indulge in behaviour and ways of being which are what we are trying to change in the first place, so long as this is done in awareness. This isn't some way of allowing ourselves to then revert back to an automatic process we've paid no conscious attention to – it's important to remember we're only human and to watch out for such natural self-sabotage. Working with the mind overlaps nicely with motivation and goal-setting, because in a space of heightened awareness we can be aware of negative focus like this and empower our aim with greater positive intention. Whilst we aspire to positive transformation in this way, it's important to inspire ourselves, through continued learning and guidance, to stay motivated in our aims (also thought of as reinforcing our belief by adding powerful references)[6]. With this in mind **Appendix 5) Self-awareness & self-talk** details a free mindful tool for mapping out our aspiration, inspirations and motivation, which is available through the WWTM community online.

Because we subconsciously cling to the ideas we have about ourselves and these ideas adhere closely to our core values and beliefs, processes of working with the mind are important to generate a concentrated state of mind[7] for clearer insight into our particular values in life at that point. This helps us to see clearer what kind of a person we feel we are, our self-beliefs that have become formed through repetition and familiarity, and how our values shape our intentions in life (whether deliberately or subconsciously and automatically).

Although it may seem hard to grasp at first, motivation helps us consider what's important to us, then to think about why it's important. Many of us don't really know our values and even those of us who feel we do, probably haven't truly looked openly at the current reasons behind the values and virtues we have, and decided what we would like to do about them. All our values, whether consciously formed or subconsciously conditioned, form the basis for why we live the way we do, and what direction in life we tend towards. We can all say I want love, that's important to me, or I want a bigger house, flashier car and so on, but what these represent to us are actually quite different from just the thing itself. However this takes some real introspection which will reveal to us our best and worst attributes – something quite difficult for many of us, especially if we are already suffering quite significantly. The difficulties of dealing with, and just being ourselves, can be quite profound, and an awareness of our needs and values is only as empowering as we can be honest and open whilst looking at the self. A desire for more money may, on closer inspection, be about self-esteem, wanting the recognition and admiration of others, or about something completely different such as wanting to be able to make more of a positive difference in the world. Getting to the core of our beliefs about what virtues and values we truly are guided by, may take some digging and progressive self-awareness. What the mind most immediately offers up on the surface, is seldom the central truth of the matter, or our most fundamental needs. Fortunately, working with the mind develops the intuition necessary to see through many of the delusions we have in life.

People generally have very similar basic needs, even psychologically, such as needing involvement and belonging, both forms of simple dependency and love, for example[8] (see **Figure 8.0**). People are interdependent, after all, even if we are an independently-minded individual, who is very self-secure. We don't feed ourselves on food grown from our own labour, wear clothes of our own design or live in houses built by our own hands, so even the fundamentals of life are the labours of countless other people that we have been fortunate enough to benefit from. Again, think back to the glass of water, and all those we depend on to be able to simply drink it! When in love, and aware that our need for love extends in some way from our dependency on and need for others, there is the option of strengthening any relationships founded in love. Greater awareness of self is so powerful in the family unit because we react to the emotional connection between people[9], and see aspects of ourselves as they are manifested in our relationships more clearly (for example, desiring support or perhaps expecting more of the other person than we are willing to do for ourselves at times, maybe even having a go at family when we feel they are not mindful enough of our experiences, desires and preferences.)

Some of our natural reactions may be more harmful to

the relationship than what we're reacting to itself, which is something helpful to keep a mindful eye on whilst hoping to mitigate the harm we cause ourselves and our family. We're often under the impression other people are to blame for how we feel, our experience and our state of mind when actually there are many reasons for feeling the way we do. Ultimately even where another's behaviour affects us, we need to take responsibility for our feelings and not apportion blame for them. As we see more of ourselves openly and in greater awareness, we can have an improved influence over taming the wild mind, and reigning in the way we act which is harmful or contrary to our chosen direction in life. For example, as difficult situations arise in life and as we're subjected to other people's negative emotions, we tend to react automatically, and with our habitual states of mind. Alternatively, we can use our awareness and quieten the mind, to uncover the causes of the situation and see what intentions arise in us because of it. If we see we are responsible for the situation or other's emotions, we can accept our part in creating it and not exacerbate things further by how we deal with it. If we conclude we're without blame we can try and see why this situation has occurred, why the other person feels this way, and perhaps find a way to interact positively and avoid causing more suffering and adding to the difficulty. The most helpful thing may even be to do nothing and not react at all, if we can find the strength to, but this all begins with awareness! We cannot control life just as we cannot control much of our family situation or the thoughts, feelings and actions of others, but knowing ourselves this way with a mindful awareness we can avoid, undo or at least experience less suffering from much of the difficulties inherent in family life and relationships. If we don't, as we suffer we just perpetuate the states of mind that feed into and react to this, causing the cycle to continue[10].

All of existence from the macrocosmic to the microcosmic scale is pretty random – and certainly mostly beyond our immediate awareness and control. It's easy to get caught up in worrying about those bits of ourselves and our lives that we cannot have any influence over, such as what happens to us, what happens when this self-image is threatened or shattered, what goes on in the world and life around us, and how we imagine that we individually and our family should and could be. Actually, once we think about it, life is largely outside of our control, and it is empowering when we give attention to the fact we cannot control everything, because we see worrying about what we cannot influence as self-harming[11]. We can become trapped in the idea of the individual person again, and this actively limits our potential as people. As we alluded to at the beginning of the book, we've become conscious of our individual way of perceiving, rather than remaining simply conscious. Often consciousness is so beguiling because of our desires – who wouldn't want a better family situation, with less worry, challenge or suffering involved, better harmony between the more difficult of our family members and an overall easier life?! There's much in the world that, without our deliberate awareness, takes all the attention we're consciously willing to give, not to mention all the subconscious attention we apply as well. This is because the things we can focus on are in greater numbers, and are more immediately distracting and

entertaining outside than within. There is also an instinctive ease with which many areas of life, including the conscious and subconscious mind, can become cluttered,
over-complicated and draining[12].

The purpose of aiming to not continually succumb to
this cognitive processing is therefore one of not overlook-
ing the self, and to perhaps look at ourselves mindfully
from this space from time to time, which is illuminat-
ing each time depending on our outlook, experience and
expectations in life. Aspiration, inspiration and motivation
are key elements of this self-development and, very often,
these are not easy steps to take, but greater self-awareness through the practices in this book strip away much of
the difficulty in the process.

Developing our own routines, and crafting our own
habits, involves a certain level of freeing ourselves from
routines and habits that we currently observe, often gradually self-imposed upon ourselves and accumulative over
time. We don't often observe a deliberate practice of
something helpful or beneficial to us, to develop purpose-
ful and positive routines and then where this does happen,
it's often after a scare or significant life event. If we have
a radical lifestyle change to account for, trying to reverse
the symptoms and cause of such a wake-up call isn't proactively looking at life – it is reacting to it, as we are all
inclined to do. Conditioned reactions, thought processes
and ways of interacting with others and ourselves are all
part of the development we have undergone to become
who we are right now. These are so deeply ingrained
that it's easy to overlook just how conditioned our habits are and our experiences that pull on the senses[13]. For

implementing any positive change in our lives, and especially to strive towards self-development for achieving a better family balance, it's necessary to take hold of this process of development and to observe a new routine practice towards who we are to become later. In other words, we mustn't wait for something life-altering to occur before we alter how we live our life by changing our attitudes and behaviour which we can see are negative, or have a limiting effect on ourselves and our family.

This aim involves a simple process, some of which we can achieve through completing the motivation exercise worksheets free online; so we can do this first to take stock of our current set of values and virtues. We have all had the momentary intention to implement a change in life, then gone back to what we used to do and how we used to be, probably trying something new many times and not getting past a certain stage with this new endeavour. Many people struggle to stick to any new method of reasoning because they do not have clear goals[14], but why, if we really analyse this and break it down, does this happen? Brains don't function just logically, but also by how we associate with things[15], and our values drive our behaviour. If we want to resort to shouting less, for example, but 'can't' because the things we've tried haven't worked (if we've tried any), then it's time to change how we think and not what we're trying. The familiarity of interacting in conflict as we do now, and not having to really change or implement new thinking and behaviour around this, is simply greater than the fear of the current situation facing us. It is harder to stop shouting because this reaction is born of our needs and desires, perhaps to be understood and have our family members respect us, listen to us and do as we suggest in this moment. Shouting arises from emotion or frustration, where we feel we are not understood, or have a solution that no one is observing and this brings about our powerful, and ingrained states. Only an equally powerful intention can interrupt and overcome them in the moment. However, this current situation is less unacceptable to us, perhaps on some subconscious, unaware level, than having to change our ways. So really we don't progress sufficiently with our efforts because we choose, consciously or subconsciously, to stick with what's currently not bad enough to make us want to change for the better. In this regard we should be wary of what we're willing to tolerate about ourselves, such as shouting at each other for the same reasons resulting from the same situations, and continually expecting some new result.

Our current life situation is more comfortable than having to implement and accept a whole new pain and discomfort of change and embracing the unknown. So in other words we self-sabotage and 'fail' to reach our aims, and to maintain our inspiration for change, because the way things are now are OK enough, or at least not that devastating, and trying to change is difficult and unfamiliar. From the perspective of working with the mind, it's suggested where practice isn't strong enough to overcome difficulty that we need to go back and re-familiarise with the exercises, sentiment that's mirrored in more traditional settings as well[16]. Because it feels uncomfortable to be observing something new for a while, we may be inclined to return to what was normal from before, forgetting that this state of normal was what we were trying to improve upon to start with. Remember to see all change as a process, and in this regard there's no real failure until we decide or tell ourselves we 'can't' do something at all. Failure and set-backs are just learning points along the way which we have the culturally ingrained view-point of seeing as negative instead of a good thing[17]. Where we bring ourselves to truly see the current state of normal as a disastrous, devastating status quo, the pain involved in changing this is almost liberating. However if any part of our ongoing thinking, feeling, speaking and being is OK with the current state of affairs, any change towards a positive goal will be likely more of an uphill struggle, or at least be the source of our greater suffering and increase the chances of self-sabotage when we do have challenge and setbacks. This can be a hard-learned lesson, and we all like to vent frustration or complain about our difficulties, but these are preferable to us than the difficulty of changing ourselves for the better.

Starting with the idea of aspiring, we have briefly discussed the importance of needing to aspire to something because of the dangers of a lack of ambition. This can be thought of as simply allowing life to be one long, continuous autopilot, where we merely allow time to unfold without any conscious engagement or deliberate assessment of what we might change for the better about our thinking, speaking and acting to get more from life. All beings everywhere are a manifestation of consciousness, in one way or another, however this understanding sits with our individual world-view, and all people are the product of their continued, conscious decisions. With enough practice we can rely on the experience of living in this state directly, or derive inspiration from those we see in the world who do; often the people who are already successful at the thing they do. Whatever it is that they do, they are putting consciousness into active practice, and not waiting for it to happen. They think about what they do, they practice it, they do it, they talk about it, and in other areas of life they draw reference or connection to their chosen focus, they don't just do it very well and think about what didn't work, they do it better and think about what helped, and when they do it well they reflect on this until it is all consuming and ingrained into the subconscious.

The subconscious mind is interesting to watch, and it is here that we all come up against struggle, because what's hindering us is our self, drawn back into the habitual and familiar pathways of the mind. With awareness we see bits of the subconscious mind as it arises (remember **Figure 4.0**); this contains mostly what we set the conscious mind to focus on over a prolonged time. So when we glimpse a momentary snippet of a beautiful and loving family, we don't think about the difficulties they face, the hard times they failed to get along in or experience their journey of thinking about what they were doing, and trying again to aspire to build and improve their relationships with each other. Essentially we just see the end result, and probably through some immediate filter of perception which may be biased based on our understanding and experience, or a little judgemental in one way or another. When seeing things from this perspective we disempower ourselves because we are taking the approach of a negative outlook, remaining focused on what we don't have but want, as opposed to a positive frame of mind focusing on what working towards this ideal would mean for us or our family. So in aspiring to a greater, better, and more positive change, we need to ensure our outlook remains positive, and notice when our frame of mind becomes negative and our passion poisoned. 'The ability to look at and change our frames of mind is key here, to ensure that a positive focus and intention always outweighs the negative especially when we are aspiring to some change for an improved family life.

What it comes down to is when we aspire towards something, we are forming a determination to work towards achieving it, then this is a purpose we can set our minds to work towards. It's a desire to get something good from the life that we have, a decision to make a deliberate difference. This process is not to be taken lightly because it may need us to change the approach which we usually follow in order to do so. Most of the time we have half-hearted intentions which are subconsciously formed, accounting for our virtues and values, and mostly conditioned in us and not deliberately decided upon for ourselves. Making a more conscious, deliberate and positive intention, based on greater awareness of our needs as an individual and as a family, is far more powerful.

In the seductive world of streaming sites, smart phones and exponential growth in the power of games consoles and social media, we can potentially fill all our free time without even having to leave the house. Cutting back on the things that waste our precious time and mental stamina is a shock to the system, and almost an insult to suggest to some people. Just knowing that there are 24 hours in a day, and truly looking at where we spend our focused attention during these hours, can be revelatory. If we love our entertainment devices and packages that's great, but if we spend more hours of life engaged in these things than thinking about, planning and working towards something of our own, then much of our attention in life will never be our own. We find ourselves continually sub-jected to the conditioned experience based upon what the world around us fills our head with. Choosing a more com-plete balance we can still do what we love, but can realise also that there is time and attention enough to aspire to something else too. Don't live with a poverty of ambition, because ambition is an incredible tool.

How then do we inspire ourselves? This is our journey and we have to figure that out for ourselves, perhaps start-ing with the free tools in **Appendix 5) Self-awareness & self-talk**, then remembering that when we suffer we need look no further than ourselves for an in-depth understand-ing of this to find a more productive way to live with the inevitable difficulties we face from time to time. Working with the mind is a most effective way for us to do this, as the process continually reveals a greater self-awareness that can punctuate even the most troubling of our states of mind, and allows us a less-disturbed, more distanced perspective on family challenges.

Inspiration to better ourselves and the world around us can come from many different sources throughout life. If we think about our concept of ourselves from a few years ago, how we see ourselves now, and where we may con-sider ourselves to be in a few years' time, the difference is obvious. Observing the ephemeral, changeable nature of all the things we understand and experience is key to working with the mind, because this helps us shatter the delusion the mind clings to – that the self is made of a constant experience and understanding[18]. Truthfully, the self is vaster than this, and change is fundamental to a balance in our approach to dealing with challenges in life through working with the mind. Change is equally important in terms of what inspires each of us, because our needs and values alter over time as greatly as we do ourselves. In this case we decide then, consciously and deliberately, to observe change and be guided by what we can be aware of, or we ignore change (and this is probably subconsciously and unintentionally) and remain ignorant of that which conditions who we see ourselves as. Both are fine, but one offers clear advantages for seeking inspiration to influence ourselves, our families and the world at large towards whatever our aim for the better. All this comes down to using our attention more effectively and responsibly. If we fail to do this, or to at least strike a balance in trying, the world and others will quickly direct our attention for us. Today our attention sells[19], and is our most powerful attribute that a product, company, organisation, person, social media platform or electronic device can capture and divert! Because we're so inept at using our attention and focus to our advantage, it's easy to unlearn the frame of mind of intrigue that we normally have naturally when we're very young, and still developing our ideas about the world. We forget that things in life are pretty amazing the more our attention is spent on the same process, thoughts and routines month after month, and year after year. With a little inspection (and introspection) we can see how much our attention is of worth to everyone outside of us, and how many would rather our focus was centred on them and the influence they wish in our lives. In this effort, what's most useful against ourselves is the resilience that grows in us as we begin to include some time spent focused, aware and more mindful of the various aspects of our daily routines. It becomes easier to look outside of our box, and to experience and understand a different perspective in life. We may naturally come to a space of wanting to break the habit of doing as we have always done, thinking as we have always thought, and getting what we have always got out of life. This essentially is seeking inspiration and allowing the world around us to be inspiring. See **Appendix 6) Bibliography** for some good places to start!

The way we're accustomed to thinking about our circumstances in life, reacting to the challenges of going through the motions of tending to our duties and responsibilities, is more difficult, negative and limiting for us than our routines, circumstances and challenges of those duties and responsibilities actually are. In learning to be more mindful we realise this through our own experiences. There is no purpose to mindful practice other than to be mindful, but the by-product of this is development of our self, a progressively greater resilience against our own natural tendency to further complicate life's difficulties. Such self-resilience is most intriguing – it helps us to notice thought, intent to act or to speak arising, then to have the ability to interrupt this pattern where it may contribute in whatever way to further difficulty and limitation. If we don't develop this ability then, as we come across that which we dislike or disapprove of, in ourselves or our experience of life, we're inclined to look away again and allow our attention to return to an uninterrupted state of autopilot (usually resulting in unhelpful emotions or out-bursts aimed at others).

For much of our early life our parents or guardian have the benefit of the supreme outside perspective, having more awareness of us than we do ourselves. This ends at the point we begin to trust in our own self-intention, more than our reliance on a parental guidance and say-so on who we are. 'Parenting' ourselves in this way however is rarely thought to be a valuable exercise; allowing an expanded outside perspective on ourselves as an individual may be something that most never even consider, and this is powerful indeed. Therefore, this is where we must learn to motivate ourselves to further our understanding and experience of working with the mind, accounting for the benefits we notice for ourselves as individuals. Included in **Appendix 4) Practice plan** is an adaptable programme to guide ongoing development and practice, and there is also more info on the working with the mind community to reach out to for support when doing this. However, without motivation these things can very easily unravel. Most of us like to eat and this is clearly helpful to do on a daily basis, we don't tend to think 'oh that was nice, I may try that again someday.' Motivation is like this, just consider what would be the outcomes if we observed time to motivate ourselves every day?!

Deciding to aspire, to find inspiration and motivate ourselves to work with the mind can be thought of as a duty or responsibility to the family and to ourselves, because developing a state of mind and a process of being more capable during the day of dealing with whatever might arise is invaluable. Setting an intention for working towards a positive frame of mind in dealing with what is expected to arise each day, is paramount in being able to come back to a responsive state of mind, following those episodes where we are affected by and negatively react to the difficulties of the day. Who we feel we know ourselves to be is a perspective that we can step outside of, which is especially useful in transforming the mind from its present state, because we cannot necessarily control the people, situations, feelings and thoughts that come about in life. What we can control is what we're aware of, where we choose to place our attention and then how we choose to respond to what happens more creatively, expanding our understanding of self and our life skills.

Regardless of what we tend to focus on in life most often, it is the attention that alters our perception of what we're focused on, and how we feel and think about it. This is so useful within the realms of family life, because by building our awareness of mind we naturally begin to notice more clearly when our focus on family is negative. For example, when we see situations where family members are annoying us, what we want from them is to stop doing whatever it is that is annoying us, but that is what's wrong *from our perspective*, a judgement based on our feelings and intentions. Our thoughts can become quite negative if all we do is think how this family member always does this and never does that, and our focus is solely on what is wrong, how it is bad, how difficult or frustrating it is. This is a rather negative angle to manage the situation from, even where we are the affronted party.

Having an awareness of the fact that it is difficult, but also an awareness, acceptance and allowance of how we may be inclined ourselves towards dealing with this in a negative way, is a powerful position to work from. Therein lies opportunity for us to try something else, to work with dealing with the same situations with a different frame of mind, by acknowledging we can try something else and come to appreciate difficulty as the opportunity to do so.

Within every family each of us start with the same basic needs as each other. We may have loosely similar desires arising from these also, but our values and virtues are our own, and our subsequent thinking, speaking and behaviour is unique to each of us. Ultimately, for our family experience to improve we need only use the skills gained through the exercises introduced in this book, to divert a little more attention and energy to a positive intention towards associating with family and those in our lives – and to know that they don't have to be the same as us for us to honour them for who they are! The most wonderful thing about working with the mind is that we don't actively have to set out with an aim to start with – if the need to aspire, inspire and motivate ourselves seems overwhelming, confusing or out of reach, we need only stick to the exercises! In a short space of time a clarity of mind arises which will enable greater awareness of where attention is needed, and this ambition can unfold progressively of its own accord. Such intuitive wisdom continually arises as we deepen our practice, much like the compassion and gratitude does from following the exercises to come in the next chapter.

Continuing practice

You can search throughout the entire universe for someone who is more deserving of you love and affection than you are yourself, and that person is not to be found anywhere.

You yourself, as much as anybody in the entire universe deserve your love and affection.

*H*ow do we bring ourselves to find space in a busy, often negatively-focused mind for attention on feeling good about ourselves, life and others? This can perhaps seem a little too far down the rabbit hole, impractical or just too far outside our comfort zone to start with. After all reflecting on gratitude, compassion, love or kindness is not a very common practice, culturally-speaking, and often those who actively promote this are either living far from our reality, testing our resolve with their unwelcome religious views or trying to sell us their version of self-development when we're fine as we are thank you very much. In this final chapter we will introduce some exercises which utilise the principles and practices covered so far, and include an anchor on positive attention through kindness, compassion and gratitude. As we always allude to in working with the mind, we have to find our own position on this, and the benefits which can be experienced are unique to us individually.

To start with, it's important to be able to remain present with difficulty so it can be transformed through positive attention and awareness. Therefore, the first practice we'll cover starts with allowing some awareness of dealing with difficulty, then we'll move onto generating kindness and gratitude. The various phenomena of the mind that are connected to our states of health and well-being, such as stress, anxiety, depression and powerful negative emotions, are not cured nor should we seek for a cure and eradication of them. Anxious, depressed, stressed and emotionally-charged states of mind are naturally occurring elements of who we are and how we engage with life. Stress, anxiety, depression and emotional or behavioural difficulties become disorders when these traits and the process of how we represent things, have become a hindrance in our daily life. In other words we can't complete our normal routines because we're overwhelmed beyond a point we can control, even if only very briefly, and everything regarded as normal becomes too difficult to manage. So, we are better served to think of this process of working with the mind whilst dealing with these phenomena not as healing necessarily, but as a means of coming to better manage the experience of living with what's inherently difficult (which ironically is restorative in itself). Because we don't ever get rid of the process of experiencing states of mind that we have, including where these are negative, irregular and overwhelming, experiencing these openly, honestly, and seeing what triggers them, how we react to them and how this influences ourselves and the world around us, is key to developing our understanding and experience. Many seasoned mindfulness practitioners, and well-known proponents of traditional or religious use of such exercises, proclaim that there is no 'way to happiness' because happiness itself *is* 'the way'. Contrarily, it's suggested here that happiness involves developing more positive qualities and attitudes, for our and others' benefit, and that this way of happiness is more a continued process of deeper familiarity with those aspects of our individual self that prohibit meaningful and prolonged happiness. By working with what's challenging to us, not ignoring or wishing it away as we do this, we avoid compounding the difficulty and desire that exacerbates the potential harm of what we find to be challenging in life.

There's nothing quite as valuable in life as upholding the

brief but routine observance of some reading, learning or practice that accumulates over time. It's through this process that we progressively develop the ability to do all of the fundamental things in life, and if we look carefully we can see the truth of this. Understanding and experiencing our own mind is fundamental to family life, and through working with the mind we progressively develop some of the most overlooked values and virtues we can instil in ourselves and others – those aspects that are vital for our own well-being, for others in our family and profoundly lacking in society in general. Values such as love and compassion are sorely missing from our family today because we don't allow ourselves to develop them in ourselves first, and these certainly aren't routinely encouraged or enabled through conventional society and its expectations on individuals.

We don't expect the experience of a difficult frame of mind to disappear, because the expectation that they do brings further suffering or difficulty when the inevitable negative frame of mind arises in life. If our attention is on ridding ourselves of inherent suffering, even if only subconsciously so, we expend our energy and effort on feeling bad about what's there, disempowering ourselves from positive change. Ironically it's the process of working with our challenging frames of mind that develops the positive attributes and attitudes to help us deal with them. Trying to determine what life is like without certain frames of mind is an unrealistic expectation which can add to their inherent hardship, and the belief that we shouldn't have to feel a certain way. However, if it is actually our experience of life at that point perhaps we should feel this way, and

this present moment difficulty may just be the opportunity we need to come to practice love, kindness, compassion, patience and tolerance (for ourselves and also for
others)! Therefore, we need to start to learn to look at the
mind, whatever is there and however it feels, rather than
expect the contents of the mind to change, or to have the
stuff we don't like there to disappear through some immediate means. This altered perspective comes simply from
the continued building on the exercises of attention and
awareness.

Paying attention to experience and understanding is a
huge undertaking, and a very significant task which we will
see the value of as we become more comfortable doing
it. This is important because developing an all-round balanced, healthy, happy family involves supporting, educat-
ing, guiding and understanding, and at times observing
the discipline of ourselves as well as expecting it others.
There's so much to just being our individual self in each
moment that the agitated, fractured attention of the day
tends to muddle and complicate matters. The mindful
process helps us to watch and allow the settling of our
thoughts, our judgements, what's happened, what we may
be working towards, how we're feeling about this particular day, any sensations in the body, and the outcomes of
our reactions to all of these. We start our practice moving
forward with a period of just a few moments for tending
to this settling process, something that's quite significant
for the positive outcomes of regularly doing working with
the mind exercises that we'll cover now.

The exercises detailed in this chapter are considered to be more advanced practices, and assume some

competence in our understanding and experience thus far. It is worth pointing out that all the obstacles to practice, and difficulties getting to grips with each progressive exercise, are far more easily overcome with some direct guidance and support – so do not despair during any difficulty with practice because this is natural. The exercises laid out in this book will test every reader at some stage, because we will have to look at ourselves deeply whilst doing these. Many of these are only taught in courses where the participants have indicated some previous level of understanding and experience through previous training and guided learning. Once we've finished with the core content of this book, there is some further information in **Appendix 4) Practice plan** at the end, which guides some on-going practice and shows us how to access further support. It's important to be able to develop, deepen and strengthen our awareness practices because as we grow progressively more competent at establishing such states of mind, we can use them therapeutically and in dealing with increasingly challenging circumstances and states of mind and conflicts in life as shown in **Figure 9.0**.

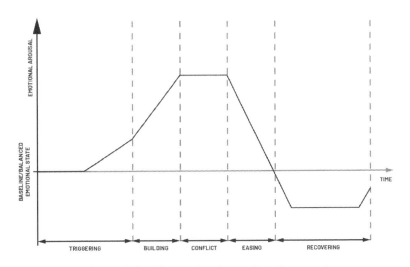

Figure 9.0 – The cycle of emotional arousal

We can review a past difficult situation, or engage our efforts immediately in the present moment whilst these scenarios unfold, and both are equally practical and achievable with a little practice establishing our own unique understanding and experiencing of working with the mind. However, it can be tricky to notice difficulty arising in the moment until a point of conflict, but this point actually only comes after a process of triggering and building of emotion and intent within us (as represented by the above **figure**). With greater awareness of our own emotional arousal and baseline emotional states, which develops through greater self-awareness from being increasingly more mindful in life (and practicing mindfulness), we see how conflict arises and affects us – regardless of the situation or circumstance. We can notice the indicators of how we react to conflict arise within us,

before finding ourselves in a state of detrimentally reacting to it. Progressive understanding and experience of
our functional range, or within what 'levels' of emotional
arousal we can still function and remain positive and productive as a person, brings with it the ability to cope better
with situations when we are tested – and there are plenty
of those in family life! The easing and recovering after
conflict, back to a balance shown in the graph, becomes
quicker when we have a mindful skill-set to check ourselves against and to intervene in negative habits as they
unfold (remember also **Figure 4.1** showing the same trend
in brain regions of non-meditators and experienced mindfulness practitioners).

For some of us, the next few practices may be quite
challenging in and of themselves, because we build in
more anchors, move attention between ideas and focus
points that are emotive, and some touch on ideas and
concepts that may be uncommon to sit and be present
with. The difficulty, compassion and gratitude exercises
that follow form some of the most powerful and transformative of the practices for working with the mind, but
also, these may appear initially elusive to some of us. Take
some time here to go over these a few times until familiar,
and remember not to hold any judgement or expectation in
mind when running through these exercises. All the practices in this book have many forms, and can be adapted
accordingly. The practices we come to now step beyond
establishing and deepening our awareness, and here we
begin to use the mindful outlook and space of heightened awareness cultivated, to look at or reflect on some
aspect of ourselves or our experience. In the **Dealing with**

227

Difficulty exercise this involves looking at that which we find challenging from a focused awareness perspective, and using a deliberate positive focus to contrast this, not to rid ourselves of difficulty but to perhaps observe what arises as we focus on it.

Before starting the next exercise, we need to consider something that is frustrating for us at present, or that's happened before that we can recall now. Perhaps something unfinished, or some confrontation or conflict that left us with the sense of it remaining unresolved after the situation ended. Whatever difficulty we bring to mind, it should not be so overwhelming or disturbing that we cannot sit with it in mind, holding some focused thought and attention on it for a few minutes. The point of the exercise is not to bring to mind something that is so overwhelming that we cannot allow any attention on it without uncontrollable suffering or difficulty! However, we are well served in finding something that does tug at our negative tendencies of mind so that we can observe what comes into mind as we watch this. Therefore, finding our own balance is important. Whilst doing the practice it's important not to get caught up in finding or sticking with particular examples of something challenging. The mind is very busy sometimes, and at other times can be very still and calm – so if difficulty doesn't come or stay long enough to reflect on, we just sit with what's present and reflect on hardship generally. Holding a difficulty in mind whilst approaching practice opens up our awareness to how we are inclined to react to challenge and confrontation. Steps to follow during the remaining exercises in the book are laid out, but remember to make use of the guided audios that are available. Take some time for each of the steps, until feeling more comfortable and familiar to extend this gradually and without the audio. Perhaps read through the steps first, to gain an understanding of what the practice involves, then follow the guided audio practice without the book. To start with, these exercises may work best if you find somewhere to sit where you can be uninterrupted for a few minutes, then with greater familiarity these can be used less formally and adapted into real-life situations.

Dealing with Difficulty

- Sitting for a few minutes focusing on the sensations of breathing. Just being aware of where the breath is most noticeable as it comes and goes.

- What sensations can be noticed as the air comes in, and as the air goes out? When it feels comfortable, widening the sense of awareness to take in the body as a whole. Perhaps lengthening the breath, breathing as deeply, and as slowly as it feels comfortable to.

- Scanning the body, and any sensations that can be noticed, breath by breath. Starting with the feet, observing the weight of the body in connection with the floor through the feet. Noticing the sitting muscles, and any pressure or support where the body is seated or standing. Feeling the shoulders and neck, is the back upright, relaxed not too tense? Is the chin slightly tucked in? Shoulders open and not slouched? Allowing the attention to settle into the body and connect to the movements of the breath, perhaps deliberately deepening the cycle of each in and out-breath.

- When noticing that attention is pulled away to thoughts, or emotions arise, exploring something different now from what we have been practicing up until this point. Instruction has been simply to notice where the mind 'goes' whilst distracted, then to gently and firmly escort it back to an anchor.

- Exploring now a different way to respond: instead of bringing the attention back from a thought or a feeling, allowing awareness of this to remain in the mind, breathing and staying present with it. Having explored this thought, sensation or feeling, shifting attention into the body; scanning with awareness for any physical sensations present that may have come along with the thought or emotion.

- This practice is especially useful for repetitive painful or difficult thoughts, feelings and emotions. Just noticing these if and when they arise, and allowing attention on them to remain in the mind, simply observing them in the present.

- Observing and noticing anywhere in the body where physical sensations can be felt, deliberately moving the focus of attention to the body where sensations maybe strongest or most noticeable.

- Perhaps imagining, as we have practiced, breathing into this region of the body. Breathing out from it on the out breath. This time not to change the sensations present but to explore them, seeing them clearly, really heightening and tuning into the experience of this sensation with each breath. Noticing any connection to any thoughts or difficult feelings, memories, emotions that have come and are present in this moment.

- Just exploring this sensation in sync with the breath. Where no difficulties, concerns or challenging emotions and thoughts arise, perhaps if it feels comfortable deliberately bringing to mind a challenge or difficulty that's relevant in life at the moment.

- Reflecting on this, does it feel unpleasant? Unresolved? Perhaps a misunderstanding, conflict or argument, situation involving the feeling of anger or regret over something that's happened.

- Bringing these situations to mind now just noticing any thoughts or feelings arise with it. Scanning the body for where the most noticeable sensations are, whilst allowing the mind to reflect on, and delve further into this 'story of difficulty'.

- Allowing time to tune into any physical sensations in the body. If no significant noticeable body sensations or emotional charge arise then focusing on the movements connected to the breath. Really filling the awareness with just these sensations, deliberately directing the focus of attention to the region of the body where these sensations are present.

- Bringing to this practice a feeling of a gesture of an embrace, of welcoming what's present, not turning from any sensations that are present or pushing away any of the feelings or memories that arise in connection to this difficulty.

- Perhaps breathing into the part of the body on the in breath, and breathing out from the region on the out-breath. Exploring the sensations watching any intensity shift up and down, from one moment to the next.

- Setting attention on any body sensations present, unpleasant or pleasant, deepening this attitude of acceptance, of openness to whatever sensations are present.

- Honestly experiencing just in the present moment. Perhaps thinking 'This experience is present and it's ok to be open to it, whatever it is, it's already there.'

- Softening and opening up to the sensations present in this moment. Intentionally letting go of any tensing or bracing. Seeing if it's possible to stay with the awareness exploring these body sensations and any affects that arise because of them.

- Breathing with them in a spirit of acceptance. Letting them be here, allowing them just as they are. If anything feels 'wrong' or 'right' still just allowing, simply being in awareness of that feeling.

- Right now remaining open to the sensations present in the body connected to bringing this difficult situation to mind. There doesn't have to be a like for these feelings, it's perhaps not natural to want to have unpleasant thoughts or sensations.

- Maybe saying inwardly: 'These feelings are part of the present experience only, and not the whole of the experience'. It's ok not to want these feelings, but they are already here, so just be open to them.

- Perhaps experimenting with holding in awareness both the sensations in the body, and the feeling of breath moving in and out. Breathing with the sensations moment by moment.

- And sitting with this difficult situation in mind for a few more cycles of breath, noticing any other feelings or sensations that become present. Noticing the body sensations are no longer pulling attention to the same degree, settling the focus back onto the breath as it comes and goes.

- Releasing awareness and focus of any difficulty or painful thought and emotion. Deliberately following the breath, breathing as deeply as it is comfortable to, all the way in, and all the way out. When it feels comfortable just gently open the eyes or raising the gaze.

The opportunity for reflection on our inter-connectedness discussed in previous chapters, comes into its own in the **Dealing with Difficulty** exercise. Considering the suffering of ourselves and then others, is a natural precursor to being able to begin compassion or kindness exercises because we can wish more sincerely to ease suffering once we reflect on the inherent nature of difficulty that we all face in one form or another. Doing this exercise becomes progressively easier to use as challenges arise, and not just in hindsight reflecting back after the event. A focus on the links in the chain of difficult and challenging states of mind is useful to excise those links that can be transformed and replaced by a positive one instead. The practices we'll come to now are the beginnings of this process of positive change, a path of practice enabling the process of noticing difficulty as key to our transformation, from where how we chose to respond becomes something we can influence in new ways, and plan for a positive change in.

Generating Kindness

- Sitting for a few minutes focusing on the sensations of breathing. Just being aware of where the breath is most noticeable as it comes and goes.

- What sensations can be noticed as the air comes in, and as the air goes out? When it feels comfortable, widening the sense of awareness to take in the body as a whole. Perhaps lengthening the breath, breathing as deeply, and as slowly as it feels comfortable to.

- Scanning the body, and any sensations that can be noticed, breath by breath. Starting with the feet, observing the weight of the body in connection with the floor through the feet. Noticing the sitting muscles, and any pressure or support where the body is seated or standing. Feeling the shoulders and neck, is the back upright, relaxed not too tense? Is the chin slightly tucked in? Shoulders open and not slouched? Allowing the attention to settle into the body and connect to the movements of the breath, perhaps deliberately deepening the cycle of each in and out-breath.

- Bearing in mind the intention for developing these attributes of mind, of coming to reflect on kindness for our self and for others, whatever arises. If resistance comes up, feelings of awkwardness, just seeing these as they are.

- Bringing the attention gently to the centre of the chest, perhaps feeling a slight expansion here when the breath enters and a contraction when it leaves. Lengthening and deepening the breath to as far as it will comfortably go, noticing these sensations again; a gradual rising of the chest on the in breath, and falling on the out breath.

- If it helps to identify this area, placing a hand on the centre of the chest whilst taking some slow deep breaths, feeling the sensations in the chest area as the breath comes and goes.

- Whilst maintaining a focus on this breathing, softly bringing to mind a visual image of our self. Keeping the breath relaxed, quiet, smooth and deep see what images arise in the mind when thinking of the self. Is there a clear image of the face? Perhaps more of the body included in the image. Is it moving or still as if from a photo? Shift the focus of awareness onto any feelings that arise with the images, observing these for a moment. Where no images or associated feelings come to mind, or where thoughts and other sensations arise more predominantly, simply bringing the attention back to the sensations of breathing in the centre of the chest.

- On an in-breath, gently noticing the muscles around the face, bringing attention to the whole of the face and head on the outbreath. Are the muscles tight? Relaxed? Is the mouth slightly open or firmly closed?

Being aware of any sensations in the face whilst gently releasing the corners of the mouth if they're held closed, slightly parting the lips. Do the muscles smile naturally, does it feel awkward or forced, perhaps playful? Noting any thoughts or feelings arising in the mind, staying with awareness of how this feels. Then gently releasing the facial muscles, relaxing the awareness for a moment.

• Focusing the attention back on the breath, what sensations are in the chest whilst slowly, deeply breathing in and out. Noticing a natural pause between each cycle of the breath. Bringing to mind an image of the self again, seeing the face smile subtly, contentedly, perhaps in a state of happiness and joy – maybe grinning an obvious or amusing cartoon smile with over-exaggerated features! How does this feel? What comes to mind when concentrating on whatever images arise most easily?

• Just breathing, whilst exploring the image of our self – is it clear, can the eyes be seen, is the whole image in focus – or different parts of the face more pronounced than others? Focusing awareness again on how this feels. Gently escorting attention back to the centre of the chest; and the movements of the breath.

• Expanding this space of awareness from the chest, to notice the whole of the body, scanning for any noises present, a heartbeat, rustle of clothing, swallowing or sound of air moving in and out of the lungs. Expanding the focus to the room, and the space of awareness around the body, listening, noticing. Outside of the room and as far as possible; scanning for any other sounds present. Just sitting aware of the coming and going of any sounds that can be heard, checking occasionally that the breath is deep and rhythmical, generating a repetitive sound or sensation as the air flow enters and leaves the body. In this deeper state of awareness reflecting on some positive qualities about our self, acts of kindness, things we're good at, people who rely on us; what is it like to be who we are? Is it easy to bring to mind a positive quality, do other thoughts, emotions or sensations arise? When aware that the focus has slipped from our positive qualities, bringing the attention back to the steady sound of breath flowing in and out, and the ambient sounds of the room, just breathing and listening.

- On the next out-breath, allowing a positive statement about the self to come to mind. On the in-breath refining or repeating this statement, and repeating this process for the cycle of a few breaths. If nothing particular comes to mind, perhaps starting with 'may I be happy' or 'may I be free from suffering'; and see what adaptations of these arise naturally allowing the mind to explore this idea of kindness.

- Gently scanning the awareness for any thoughts, feelings or other sensations that arise about this practice, and returning the focus to a soft scanning for sounds in the room around, and within the body.

- Slowly releasing the focus of this practice, and gently bringing awareness to the space the body is in. Perhaps sitting if it is comfortable after opening the eyes, in this space having completed the loving kindness exercise. Expecting the chime to signal the end of practice, seeing if awareness can be brought to the entire sound, anticipating it before it comes, and maintaining awareness of the sound from the very first vibrations reaching our ears until it dissipates.

Visualising, reflecting and repeating this exercise arouses positive feelings of loving-kindness. Whichever method is most effective to arouse a positive feeling, that feeling becomes the primary focus. Keep the mind fixed between these anchors as it strays, stimulating the mind's focused attention on kindness (and also be sure to refer to the **appendix** for details on accessing further exercises available).

Grateful Thoughts

- Sitting for a few minutes focusing on the sensations of breathing. Just being aware of where the breath is most noticeable as it comes and goes.

- What sensations can be noticed as the air comes in, and as the air goes out? When it feels comfortable, widening the sense of awareness to take in the body as a whole. Perhaps lengthening the breath, breathing as deeply, and as slowly as it feels comfortable to.

- Scanning the body, and any sensations that can be noticed, breath by breath. Starting with the feet, observing the weight of the body in connection with the floor through the feet. Noticing the sitting muscles, and any pressure or support where the body is seated or standing. Feeling the shoulders and neck, is the back upright, relaxed not too tense? Is the chin slightly tucked in? Shoulders open and not slouched? Allowing the attention to settle into the body and connect to the movements of the breath, perhaps deliberately deepening the cycle of each in and out-breath.

- Allowing an awareness of the bodys surroundings to take a back-seat in the mind, and concentrating on the flow of breath as it arrives into, and as it leaves the body – noting any sensations and feelings that are connected to this.

- Bringing to mind a sense of appreciation for all that is present in this space of awareness, thinking or saying 'thank you for this breath, thank you for this body, thank you for this space of awareness' Supplementing with your own words where this is more comfortable, and repeating this cycle, matching each phrase to flow of the breath 'thank you for this breath'. 'Thank you for this body'. 'Thank you for this space of awareness'.

- Focusing on the bodys surroundings, expanding awareness to include objects of the senses; smelling, tasting, touching, seeing, hearing. Experiencing the present moment as what can be perceived through the senses. Bringing to mind a sense of appreciation for all that is present in the space of awareness, thinking or saying 'I am grateful for this sense of smell, and all that I can smell. I am grateful for this sense of taste, and all that I can taste. I am grateful for this sense of touch, and all the physical sensations I can percieve. I am grateful for this sense of sight, and all the things that I can see. I am grateful for this sense of hearing, and all the things that I can hear.'

- Supplementing with your own words where this is more comfortable, and repeating this cycle, matching each phrase to the flow of the breath 'Thank you for this sense of smell, and all that I can smell. Thank you for this sense of taste, and all that I can taste. Thank you for this sense of touch, and all the physical sensations I can perceive. Thank you for this sense of sight, and all the things that I can see. Thank you for this sense of hearing, and all the things that I can hear.'

- Focusing awareness onto thoughts of the people in our life, observing what comes into the mind as we think about family, friends, colleagues, acquaintances, parents, teachers, bosses, employees, strangers; anyone in our life that memory or thought of arises in the mind. Bringing to mind a sense of appreciation for these thoughts, memories and sensations that arise focusing in this way, and all that is present in the space of awareness.

- Thinking or saying 'thank you for the people and the relationships in my life, good or bad they all have contributed to making me who I am'. Supplementing with your own words where this is more comfortable, and repeating this cycle, matching each phrase to the flow of the breath 'thank you for the people and the relationships in my life, good or bad they all have contributed to making me who I am'. Supplementing with your own words where this is more comfortable, and repeating the cycle; matching each phrase to the flow of the breath.

- Bringing awareness to focus onto the breath, and any sensations in the body, concentrating the attention where the most noticeable sensations are. Just breathing, residing in this moment, perhaps aware of a sense of appreciation for all that is present in the space of awareness, including thoughts, opinions or sensations that that we've noticed during this practice. Allowing these, and anything else that arises to come and to go, just focusing on the flow of breath into, and out of the body.

- If at any point noticing that we have become caught up in a chain of thought, adding to the story of what arises, just gently escorting the focus back to the breath, expressing gratitude for being able to notice the distraction of the mind during this practice.

- When it feels comfortable, slowly releasing anything held in focus in the mind, relaxing the body and opening the eyes when comfortable, perhaps just sitting for a moment allowing awareness to expand to take in the room and surroundings in this space of gratefulness before continuing with the day.

Don't forget that these can be complicated practices, and that it's important to adapt these exercises after some familiarity with them. Using these practices routinely can be tricky to fit into busy family routines to begin with, whether we already have an established mindfulness practice or not. Having read the book make sure to reach out to the online community Facebook page @

mindbehindbars for support in finding your own balance in understanding and experiencing this, and with personalising these exercises. The next chapter recaps the key learning points from this title in the Working With the Mind Series, and can be used as daily inspiration for practice – open the chapter at any page for a few lines of inspiration and motivation! Do not forget that working with the mind must ultimately be for ourselves, even though we may also do this to better our family life and experience. We are well served by keeping in mind the advice that we owe ourselves love as much as anyone else.

If you have found this book beneficial in any way, we only hope that it has supported you to develop your understanding and experience of mindfulness principles, and of all things working with the mind! The Working with the Mind Series was developed to support mindfulness-based community projects, and we're continually seeking to adapt and update them accordingly. Any and all feedback is welcome (contact us through the community group – see Appendix 1) Further support), and we look forward to hearing from you in the WWTM community where you can ask any questions and access more free support and further services.

A book in brief

*L*ife is challenging and awareness of this helps with family life! As we use our deliberate attention wisely, these challenges become less overwhelming and help us navigate the difficulty of family and everyday life. Without deliberate attention, our subconscious mental states that are limiting or harmful are left unchecked and it's easier to get overwhelmed by frames of mind we're unaware of. A more mindful outlook is helpful here, which we understand and experience for ourselves by using attention and awareness. This becomes very useful during challenging moments, because it is awkward to have awareness of difficulty.

Working with the mind shines a light on our normal distracted states, and that attention is subconsciously and automatically directed. Negative habits and states proliferate under autopilot where there's no deliberate attention, which is why a mindful perspective is beneficial because it punctuates this autopilot, helping identify situations, circumstances and their effects on us.

Attention is limited and isn't easy to use, but by noticing this and exercising attention, we're able to look at challenging circumstances in family life instead of avoiding and ignoring them. We notice more about ourselves and life by using awareness and attention, and can observe patterns of thinking and reacting, noticing characteristics and situations we would have reacted to strongly before.

Mindful processes help influence our states of mind, and empowers us to be responsible instead of looking for someone or something to blame. When feeling bad about ourselves and things that happen (inevitable in life from time to time), we can notice these as feelings not as fact. Truth is only true via our own interpretation, and in taking experiences less personally we breed less negativity in the mind.

Perception and sense are reactive and we're engaged with them before being aware of them. Mindfully we can wholesomely respond to sensory information interpreted by the brain, rather than react to it. Centring our attention on the self, not letting it wander between what's going on in and around the self, we notice conditioned reactions in the mind – and spark off the beginning of new neural pathways and habits.

Despite the extent of our understanding of the mind today, we still lead lives dominated mainly by awareness of the extrinsic physical nature of reality. The consequence of this for family and daily life is that attention is drawn to the challenging aspects. Focus on the negative becomes deeply ingrained in our interactions and reflections within family and ourselves. Through more open-mindedness we see that we do not need to fix such challenges, merely to not add further suffering to them.

By anchoring attention we are deliberately aware, non-reactive, and are just watching the mind in each moment. We see the mind's natural process of internalising sensations, and the bias of how it relates to ourselves. Progressively externalising these sensory phenomena, we reduce the harmful effects of a sense of self-attachment. Regardless of experience and understanding, greater competence begins with noticing our current incompetence, and working with the mind is a cycle, not an end result.

We are what we repeatedly do.
Excellence then is not an act, but a habit.

We each assume how we think, speak and act in life is normal, but 'normal' is familiarity and repetition, and what is considered 'normal' varies from one person to the next. Our status quo isn't always healthy or balanced for ourselves or our families. If we continue to do what is normal we don't develop, so to improve our family situation we first place attention on the effects of our own routine states. We see our role in situations that are challenging, can perceive our own annoyance, and notice the other's difficulties. Allowing ourselves to be present, we draw back from automatic perception of these situations, then thought, speech and reactions can be observed. We see our inclination to respond to situations, and this observant state of mind is useful as we notice 'just being' is hard, and we see how our attention continually gets drawn towards doing not observing.

With heightened awareness, experiences are less disruptive and taken less personally. Allowing our experience develops intuition, helping us to be present and accept circumstances (even the difficult ones). Working with the mind disrupts the habitual, negative reactions to others and situations, enabling an experiential, not cognitive state of mind. This can be thought of as being in the moment not thinking about or reacting to it.

Even subconsciously, we seek gratification and avoid discomfort, so being present and allowing attention on what's challenging can be difficult. As we determine consciously that we shouldn't have to feel bad, we miss the opportunity to learn and develop from difficult situations and family conflict. Instead of being caught up in feeling bad, it's wiser to accept difficulty as natural, then we notice as we react to the detriment of our family and ourselves.

We often cling to our edited version of ourselves and others, oblivious to traits we disapprove of and focused on those we like. Seeing more openly than this, through an expanded perspective, we can see ourselves, family and life through greater awareness. Accepting the negative ways we affect ourselves and our family helps, because *what we do* about what happens in life is more important than *what happens* in life.

It's good to notice the discomfort in life, as it helps challenge the mind's avoidance tendency. Reflecting on why we recoil from that which makes us ill at ease, we learn to look at ourselves more deeply. We progressively develop our self-awareness and self-control. Maintaining awareness of mind in everyday life and transforming a negative or reactionary state of mind, becomes easier.

We shouldn't seek to remove suffering or challenge from life, but to deal with it. This transformation is not positive thinking, but a way to acceptance, not avoidance, of what we face. Observing negative habitual responses, involves looking at thoughts, emotions and feelings, then at how we speak and act as a result. From here we reflect on how we wish to respond differently.

Remember that we see the world as *we are*, not as *it is*, and if we aim for positive outcomes for ourselves and our family we need only develop ourselves and our perspective of the world follows. In this sense, acceptance of our states of mind has a greater potential to change our lives, than any attempts to change our situations in life or other's behaviour do.

What we want is important, but accepting life as it is now is vital. Understanding and experience of both comes through awareness, attention, allowing and accepting, whereas normally we have little awareness of what we truly want and how we'd rather respond to life. We cognitively associate most strongly with our subconscious expectations which we can't immediately control, and this impacts upon family situations and how we experience life. As we sustain attention over time we notice that life changes regardless of our intent and expectations. So greater acceptance of the nature of mind enables us to appreciate the perspective of others, even if we don't agree with it or are affected by it, and helps us come to accept ourselves and others more easily.

The world as we have created it is a process of our thinking.
It cannot be changed without changing our thinking.

It's important to manage expectations whilst practicing mindfulness, because heightened awareness of difficult, hurtful and traumatic experiences can be challenging. Although enjoying practice isn't key to benefiting from it, we need not harm ourselves in order to practice! Enquiry after practice through community to support this is help-ful where practical.

Mindfulness requires repetition and familiarity, and ini-tially must be actively implemented (to know, but not to do, is not to know). We begin with establishing a 'space of awareness', looking at the body to exercise our attention. Then we look at the objects of perception, such as sensa-tions and thoughts. We progress to using this awareness in order to have some mindful attention of interactions with our environment and situations. The whole process is a personal experience and we'll come to our own under-standing of this through trying and adapting mindful tools and exercises.

When we are on autopilot our attention and ener-gies are scattered and we gather them by anchoring, which involves attaching our attention to a chosen point, whether an object, sound, sensation, thought or memory, for example. We start with simple anchors and progress to using different ones to suit our needs. While anchored we watch things pass through our awareness, and then continue with our focus unaffected by what we observe.

The anchors of breathing movements and bodily sen-sations are the foundation which helps to ease states of agitation and the mind to become less automatically reac-tive. Long periods of practicing or drastically changing our lives isn't necessary to notice the benefits of working with the mind. In a mindful state, we don't identify with whatever arises – we just note the experience. Remember to become familiar with the guided audio exercises for Breathing Mindfully, and the Body Scan. With body aware-ness we can listen to its needs, and note the signals it sends more clearly. The state of our body links closely to our states of mind, and in tuning into the body we work closely with the mind.

As we're forever drawn into an objective awareness greater than our awareness of self, we continually mistake what goes on in life for life itself.

We consider that which we experience as our actual, individual self, rather than something that simply happens in our life at that point.

There's always ongoing challenge in life, regardless of affluence and lifestyle. We shouldn't expect to fix or cure this, just to remember that our states of mind influence each other. Working with conscious awareness we gradually influence our subconscious mind and can experience more intuitive states that help during the difficult and heightened emotional states of everyday and family life.

Applying the first 5 steps of WWTM to aspects of ourselves that limit our family life, transitions into using the 6th step –transforming these aspects into something more positive. Reflecting on challenge, we take responsibility for getting the best out of such situations. Remember that circumstances and events are not as important or influential as what we do about them.

We can acknowledge our ingrained states of mind, and those of our family members, making greater compassion and kindness possible later. By acknowledging our own negative reactions, we can intuitively come to change these. We grow by thinking, speaking and acting contrarily to the states we notice that are limiting. By repeating self-limiting old habits we affect those around us, and ourselves in the same ways as before.

Advancing our practice takes dedication and this is a personal balance to find. Different adaptations of practices are useful for dealing with difficult partners or parents, or for noticing and holding back our own negative habits if they hurt our family. All these start with self-focus. Ultimately, we cannot change our family members, but we can alter how we are aware of and place attention in response to family situations.

Equanimity, or balanced states of mind, help us to come back to a baseline – and not overreact emotionally. Such balance is useful, because mind tends to focus on what we're feeling and how this affects us, what we think about it and how to react, instead of just on what's going on. Advancing practice and greater equanimity allows experience to be as it is and to accept difficulty as being a vital part of experience for our growth and development as a person.

Our thinking, speaking and acting is our own, and by working with the mind consistently we minimise further harm in conflict as it is present in life. This doesn't mean there's an instant change, and if you get frustrated because of the pace of progress, remember this is a gradual process.

Being responsible for that which we want in our lives and for our family, instead of continually sharing our negative characteristics with our loved ones is an ongoing *choice* to make.

Our immediate subconscious reactions are determined by our core values, desires and energetic state, meaning we want to have or to avoid certain experiences and things, and our states of mind range from apathetic to agitated, depending on our energy.

Our normal states of mind are comfortable and this familiarity is preferable in autopilot, albeit absent-minded, easily distracted, quick to temper and slow to calm. Through improved focus we hold many things in greater awareness, including the negative, without the risk of them being overwhelming to us or negatively influencing our states of mind. This helps us realise what we can and can't control in daily and family life, then to reduce harmful outcomes for ourselves and family when things don't go according to what we want or intend.

Mindful presence of mind has a more positive influence on our family than continued judgement of their actions (even when negative). Embodying things like openness, honesty and respect is something to reflect on as this helps us to manage our expectations of, and impact on, others around us.

By avoiding what's emotional and overwhelming for us, we neglect to see that true strength and stability come from noticing, not ignoring flaws. This is reflected immediately in our family dynamic, which is only ever as strong as we are individually. We allow the perceived flaws of others, because we see the extent of our own!

Family is incredibly significant to life, and without greater attention focused on it we do it and ourselves a monstrous disservice. Be wary of desiring beautiful weddings and dream houses, if in the process we neglect the attention we pay to building healthy partnerships and happy homes. In this regard moving away from 'I focus' is important to maintain our family health, because family is greater than I. Working with the mind help us to do this, and develops a less biased interpretation of what can be perceived, for this governs all our states of mind and out-comes in life.

There are no facts, only interpretations

Expecting that difficulties between us as family, or con-flicts and arguments will just get better, is like expecting the same of perceived difficulty and negative states of mind. Within family life, we must act on opportunity to grow and change, because if not, these dynamics repeat.

Appreciation removes much of the suffering inherent in seeking our desired outcomes in life, because desire is never fulfilled. It's more enjoyable and important to appreciate what we have – this means we avoid becom-ing entrapped in the ever-seeking state of mind, for-getting that happiness and success for our family is not achievement-based.

Gratitude is an anchor that helps us to see that good in life right now, even in an on-going negative experience. After all, without bad experiences, how would we learn to change or to recognise the good? Life's wonder and beauty is found in the easily over-looked aspects of it. Even a glass of water can be means of transformation, if we reflect on it with appreciation. Developing this anchor brings greater positivity, which acts as a platform from which regarding the pleasant and unpleasant as being equal becomes easier.

The pain of seeing our flaws and traumas may be why the mind disassociates so readily, and gratitude is a help-ful root to the present even if self-observance is uncom-fortable. Remember desires aren't a good measure of our happiness as an individual or family, and even if we desire freedom from our suffering, this desire becomes a root for further suffering.

So, appreciation of our own vulnerability is practical, because we can then direct kinder intention to our own self where needed. Appreciation of difficulty makes challenge something to overcome not avoid, and we can return to a less emotive, non-reactive state more easily. When this happens, working with the mind carries significant benefit for our family around us, as well as ourselves.

Gratitude brings a progressive resilience to pain, difficulty, serious trauma and grief, and helps us view these more openly. Although this isn't easy, we see through these steps that it isn't as complicated or impossible as perhaps we may think. Gratitude is the first part of a key focus on deliberately paying attention in a constructive frame of mind which helps us to heal, nurture and develop the mind.

Healing is a matter of time, but it is also sometimes a matter of opportunity.

Because it's key to adapt mindful exercises to our own needs, understanding and experience, it is helpful to set our frame of mind as we approach practice – to establish what our intention is. This stops us finding reasons not to practice, and settles the mind quicker as we start our exercise. In the same regard, moving is a helpful anchor because it can guide attention more naturally than simply following the breath. Movement anchors fit nicely into the day and can make practice feel less formal and boring. Remember to become familiar with the guided audio exercises for Moving with Awareness.

It's hard to be objective in life! Thoughts are especially

provoking but they're not facts! Because thoughts arise 'from within' we do not analyse the validity of our own thought stream. Looking at thoughts we see they're random, unfiltered and changeable, even dark, difficult and emotionally-charged ones – we see they're simply the rapid and short-lived processing and replaying of information in the mind. This can be a relief to those of us who suffer greatly with the 'truth' that our cycling thoughts tell us about life. Remember to become familiar with the guided audio exercises for Mindful of Thoughts.

Thought influences states of mind, emotions and opinions, and we are easily lost in thought without greater awareness. By practicing we see the mind ruminating incessantly, and interrupt the continued strengthening and expression of the habitual thought patterns there. This further guides us intuitively, where we negatively influence family life through our reaction-based thinking.

Autopilot is natural and can be tempting, but as we understand and experience the benefits of a mindful outlook it's natural to want to continue working with the mind. This transformation needn't be extreme or require militant reform of our family, it just involves finding balance appropriate to our needs, and overcoming the hindrances to continuing these exercises.

As research continues we understand the neural mechanisms and brain and behaviour changes observed from practice. This can help in finding a balance between understanding and experience, although we benefit from this process by the doing of it alone – even with a limited understanding.

All difficulties we face stem from an impercipience of

self.
This conditions our expectations of what should and should not happen to us in life.

It's easier to focus on the infinite and irrelevant differences between people, rather than to notice the finite and fundamental ways we're united. Compassion practice helps us see this connection, and benefits us individually, as a family and on a wider social scale. Practicing involves reflecting on ourselves or others, or speaking and acting in a way deliberately focused on some positive intention, although this needn't involve grand complicated gestures.

As long as there's the intention to reduce suffering, compassionate focus will become progressively more sincere and authentic, even if it doesn't feel so to start with. States of mind arising from a focus on affection are further positive transformational tools, useful within the family and general life for overcoming ingrained difficulty with ourselves and others.

The importance of love for family tends to be overshadowed by our tendency to get wrapped up in our self-experience and individual ideas of love because there are many forms of love and we hold different intentions behind each of them. Kindness and compassion are virtues we assume we're either bestowed with or not, yet thinking, speaking and acting determines our states of mind, so we progress to observing a deliberate focus on affection.

Choosing to observe states of mindful affection helps with the stressful, emotional and reactive situations of family life. This gradually opens us up so that recalling the understanding and experience we have from affectionate spaces of awareness, means these challenging

255

situations are less destructive even where highly charged emotionally.

We need to establish kindness towards the self, or it will be difficult to manifest this in our intention towards others. Affectionate acceptance of anger, stress and aspects of self that constrict the mind creates something positive, whereas worry and self-judgement of our own flaws continues the suffering of them.

The paradox arises with our growing awareness that consciously we wish not to feel bad, yet the negative associations within us arise from the subconscious mind automatically and incessantly. Consciously focusing on the forgiving wisdom of self-compassion, helps understanding and the experience of undoing the habitual negative subconscious through continued attention on the empowering nature of compassion.

The apparent difficulty we have with compassion is in allowing attention on negative attributes and in considering these less self-indulgently. Being oblivious to negativity allows harm to accumulate unchecked, conditioning the automatic mind while we're unaware. Gradually strengthening the pattern of compassion weakens the negative reactions growing in the mind. As we can look with greater kindness at the restricting aspects of our character, and those of family members, we see a more fulfilling way of relating to ourselves and others.

Affection strengthens values we already have, and helps us look at emotionally charged thoughts, sensations and speech. It doesn't really diminish our character in any way, but the absence of a focus on affection can be devastating – to us, to family and to humanity at large.

What we hold in conscious awareness is vital to family as this literally moulds who we are continually becoming, and in turn, the effects we have on others. Beyond family we see affection as paramount to human development, because we value using our head so much but overlook using our hearts. This continually shatters the delusions of the mind that continually grow from the roots of our current perceptions.

We experience ourselves, our thoughts and feelings as something separated from the rest, a kind of optical delusion of consciousness.
This delusion is a kind of prison for us, restricting us to our personal desires and to affection for only a few persons nearest to us.
Our task must be to free ourselves from this prison by widening our circle of compassion to embrace all living creatures and the whole of nature in its beauty and wonder.

Poverty of ambition arises in our conditioned thinking, opinions and beliefs, but this restrictive habit is also an opportunity to become more appreciative and affectionate – and more able to support as positive a family environment as practical.

It's easy for us to develop a negative focus when working towards a positive change and even our best intentions can easily become detrimental to the mind. In this sense mental well-being is forever a tilting balance, awareness of which is extremely useful. That which helps our development requires us to be open to inspiration, because our mind that's created and supports our current experience and understanding isn't wise enough to see what may be helpful to expand this further.

Maintaining awareness of our needs, desires, values and virtues helps tremendously, because unbeknownst to us, many of these develop unconsciously over time. Habitual intentions through our thinking, speaking and acting are driven by our values and virtues and we cling strongly to these intentions – nevertheless, they are changeable and we are easily swayed by desire.

As we look we see the obvious disparity between desire and need, and that our basic needs are indistinguishable between all people, regardless of individual desires. We find that it's our desires that cause difficulty and suffering, because even where our needs are met, desire remains for yet other things. As we gain a greater ability to pay attention we see our needs are fulfilled as and when they should be, and we notice our desires are forever present.

All our emotions, thoughts and feelings are fundamentally our responsibility, and it is not for us to blame anyone or anything for. Nevertheless, we do seek to blame as we're trapped in the cycle of focusing on that which is outside of our sphere of influence. When we shift this focus onto what we can control, there is no need for any blame, because we see that we contribute significantly to our own challenges in life.

Such is the distraction of our lives in the world that our attention is never where it needs to be, even within our own being, until we learn to direct it. This, paradoxically, involves learning to 'un-distract' (or focus) our mind, not to avoid distraction itself.

Working with changing ourselves in this way involves observing our routines and deliberately altering these to instigate a positive change towards a different outcome later. What we accept in life does need to be looked at, because it's not the highest but the lowest version of ourselves that we're willing to accept. By making the current version of ourselves and our habitual states of mind more unacceptable, we ease this process of change and the inherent suffering and set-backs during the process which all impact negatively on ourselves and our family.

Where we don't aspire to change, life's long autopilot dictates change for us, subject to whatever conditioned state we may be most familiar with. To put it simply, start using attention more carefully and deliberately to ensure that any change is positive and that we do not succumb to growing misery and suffering.

The practice of working with the mind is all-pervading, so where there's difficulty in our aspiration for family life, a mindful state of mind is intuitive and useful. We see the delusion that 'self' is a constant experience, and can pay attention to the areas of life better served by aspiring to positive transformation. Through mindful awareness, family life itself is inspiring, and we are moved to want to trim away the type of thinking we may have that gives birth to speaking and acting in ways which don't recognise ourselves and our family in this spirit.

Viewing others (and ourselves) indifferently is more harmful and limiting than any of the conflict, disagreement and difficult situations that arise naturally as part of everyday and family life. In this regard, our own self-resilience is infinitely valuable, and allowing an expanded, 'outside perspective' of ourselves is key.

Without motivation the best-placed intentions can

come undone, motivation therefore is best observed like a meal – enjoyed every day! To be able to recognise and alter our negative states of mind and emotions that negatively influence each other, is almost a duty to ourselves and family.

The greatest honour we can do ourselves and our family is to recognise each other, and in trying to get the better of family life, not to overly impose the harmful aspects of our individuality on others in our family unit.

It is not our purpose to become each other; it is to recognise each other, to learn to see the other and honour them for who and what they are.

Seeking perfect health, well-being or happiness is futile and causes suffering. The ebb and flow of emotional states is natural, and aiming to 'cure' the disordered, stressed, anxious, depressed, emotional mind (or to correct our family member's behaviour) should be avoided.

Learning to better managing the self-experience of life as ourselves, shouldn't be considered a fix – it is a realisation. We intrinsically have all the health, happiness and well-being needed within us, yet our nature is such that this becomes occluded in the everyday habits of life. We see this clearly when we use mindfulness to penetrate the layers of what gets caught up in the expression of self.

There is no specific way to become happy and rid ourselves of the suffering inherent in our difficult frames of mind and emotional states. Happiness itself is the way. It's through the process of working with challenge that such abilities and strengths develop that enable us to be happy - not by wishing away or ignoring the difficult. This merely exaggerates life's challenges, and the desires we have around them which in itself exacerbates any harm that we experience.

It's easy to assume that we shouldn't have to experience hardship and difficulty, but actually our suffering is key to our growth and learning. This is true for the individual, and for the family unit. Paying attention to such experience can be daunting, and it's all the easier to just allow the autopilot state of mind to run rampant! To develop more positive states of mind and to allow our experiences, establishing a settled mindful state of mind first is helpful indeed. Such a period of settling also helps while engaging in the longer exercises of working with the mind. Remember to become familiar with the guided audio exercises for Dealing with Difficulty, Generating Kindness, and Grateful Thoughts.

In a deeply attentive space of mindful awareness, all difficulty dissolves as the layers of self-identity are peeled back. While in this space of awareness we can't really have difficulty or frustration of any kind, because there is just the experience of the self without the conditioning that is attached to it – and this is where the 'problems of being a person' lie.

Even where deep mindful states are elusive, the process of applying our attention in heightened awareness is itself helpful. We can review past difficulties, or engage more openly in present challenges, establishing a powerful positive focus such as gratitude and compassion. Holding difficulty, gratitude or compassion in mind in this manner during practice opens our awareness to these aspects of the self, and the potential they have.

You can search throughout the entire universe for

261

someone who is more deserving of your love and affection than you are yourself, and that person cannot be
found anywhere.
You yourself, as much as anybody in the entire universe, deserve your love and affection.

Appendix

1) Further support

Please contact us directly for access to all the guided audio exercises and extras mentioned in this book, via the website or Facebook page @mindbehindbars. The exercises and guided audios included in this book introduce the focus and anchors needed for the entire process of coming to work with the mind, whatever our background and experience. To continue to develop our understanding and experience, ongoing practice, guidance, and support is pretty key. It is important to interact with a trained and experienced teacher, and with others who have some understanding and experience of the process. Although this isn't always easily accessible to us, there are a good amount of resources and references to start with in this book(see **Appendix 6) Bibliography** below). Also make use of the online community and platform for people to support each other and ask any questions there. Mindfulness-based courses taken face to face usually span a 4-8 week period, as a minimum to support people's development of their experience and understanding of the practices and information involved. To this end it's recommended you seek out an instructor you can learn from, and develop your own home practice to continue this development and growth. **If you have found this book beneficial in any way, we only hope that it has supported you to develop your understanding and experience of mindfulness principles, and of all things working with the mind!**

2) Standards and origins

The 6 most prevalent religions according to the most recent census data (in the UK), are Christianity, Islam, Hinduism, Sikhism, Judaism and Buddhism as the most widely followed. Each of these expounds on the principles and importance of the idea of self-knowledge – of coming to know our 'self' a little more clearly to lead a 'better' life (which just means growth, development or positive change). Most traditions (spiritual or religious) have at their root some level of this idea of being fully alive, and we have laid out below the roots of self-inquiry as it pertains to the 6 religions above. Although this book is not focused on the religious or spiritually traditional, this is a useful concept to consider because in working with our mind, and in coming to be more aware of ourselves, we are indeed touching on this idea that arises throughout different spiritual and religious traditions. If we only leave space for our own faith (or absences of), thenj we are in the process of a discrimination against others that don't fit our reference. When we observe some kind of development, or positive growth and change in ourselves we are working on the key principle that we have the power to influence something for the better (and that is ourselves). When we become more aware of what difficulties we face, how we are affected by these, and how we tend to have a bias towards expecting to experience the positive that we see and avoiding the negative – we become more fully human. We need to open up to and become gradually more accepting of that which is part of our experience of life, even if it is painful, even where it is largely projected onto us as a result of the opinions and actions of others in our lives. We cannot effect as great a change in our family dynamic or the world around us, without first looking more deeply at ourselves. This starts with the mind and working with mind is a powerful tool, regardless of whatever our personal beliefs and faith traditions may be, or the absence thereof.

The glory of God is a human being fully alive.
Prayer, meditation and contemplation opened the door of revelation at Mt.
Hira, and The Prophet received Qur'anic revelation.
In dhyana, deeper awareness of oneness through meditation is the highest
Virtue.
Simran and Naam Japo, meditation on God, is the first of the three pillars.
The zaddik is more fully human.
'Access concentration' through mindful attention is the path to awakening.

Regardless of tradition, prophets of God as we refer to them were tested, spent time in isolation and contemplation – to know themselves more clearly. We include this idea as a further resource to consider for your understanding and experience of working with the mind because it can help us to be a better Christian, Muslim, Hindu, Sikh, Jew, Buddhist (atheist or any other kind of spiritual person) – because it helps us to be more fully ourselves. Do not get caught up in division, and expending energy on which systems are correct and false – they are all both. Please note there is no intention in this series of books, or any other information, products and services of WWTM Publishing, which is intended to be taken as religious advice. Faith is a personal journey, taken to discover our own relationship with what we see as God, or the most important or highest aspects of ourselves and human life. If there is any aspect of yourself, or your religious views, which feels contradicted or conflicted through any of the information or practices introduced here, it's encouraged you hold this in awareness without needing to act upon it.

3) The steps of working with the mind

**ATTENTION   AWARENESS   ALLOWING
ACCEPTING   ACKNOWLEDGING   ADVANCING
APPRECIATION   AFFECTION   ASSOCIATING
AIMING
ADAPTING exercises and ASKING for help are considered 2 important final steps in the process, that we aim to support you with through further information, exercises, products and services available through the WWTM community.**

4) Practice plan

Run through each of the practices introduced in the book as if they were part of a course you were taking, so as to get familiar with each and maximise the benefit of them. These exercises feed into each other, and as we become more settled into an aware state of mind through one of them, other practices we try add new value and provide fresh insight. Try and keep in mind that these practices are best thought of as something to adapt into your life to suit your needs, and not as something to complete once and not come back to again. Make use of the guided audios for these (and other bonus exercises) accessible in **Appendix 1) Further support**, and there is also a free practice plan, and further support available through the online community group to complete an accredited and certificated 8-week mindfulness practice course.

5) Self awareness and self-talk

Motivation is easy in life when we feel upbeat and enthusiastic and, similarly, so is finding inspiration and having something clear and positive to aspire to. At the difficult points in life which for some of us are unfortunately more often the norm than the exception, this process is somewhat more elusive and perhaps seemingly unnecessary. No-one wants to think about motivation, setting goals and seeking positive inspiration when they are in the midst of depression, addiction, poor well-being, or undergoing high levels of anxiety and stress. This is another reason why self-awareness is so incredibly important, because it determines to what extent we can experience what happens each day openly and unfettered – in wellness or otherwise. Self-awareness also enables us to have a clearer understanding of our self-talk; and how to use this more effectively to enquire into, motivate and instruct ourselves in our aims. Reach into the community mentioned in **Appendix 1) Further support** for a free AIM tool to guide and support the process of finding aspiration, inspiration and motivation.

6) Bibliography

This book draws on a range of sources because working with the mind is such a vast topic, touching on religion, spirituality, self-improvement, health and well-being, goal-setting and motivation, to name just a few areas! The references below include research studies, books, podcasts, Netflix series, YouTube videos and webpages, so that you can find something you're comfortable with which is helpful to refer to as you develop your under-standing and experience. After all, that's the only thing this book is about.

Author's Note

[1]World Health Organisation (2001) Mental Disorders Affect 1 in 4 People [online] Available at: https://www. who.int/whr/2001/media_centre/press_release/en/ [Accessed 16.4.20]

[2]Ritchie and Roser (2018) Mental Health [online] Available at: https://ourworldindata.org/mental-health [Accessed 3.2.20]

[3]Mehta, N., (2011) Mind-body Dualism: A critique from a Health Perspective. Mens Sana Monographs **9**(1), 202-209

[4]Gendle, M., (2016) The Problem of Dualism in Modern Western Medicine. Mens Sana Monographs **14**(1), 141-151

and

Gold, J., (1985) Cartesian dualism and the current crisis in medicine – a plea for a philosophical approach.

Journal of the Royal Society of Medicine **78**, 663
[5]Bavishi, A., Slade, M., D., and Levy, B., R., (2016) A Chapter a Day – Association of Book Reading with Longevity. Social Science and Medicine **164**, 44-48

Prologue

[1]Flynn, F., J., (2005) Having and Open Mind: The Impact of Openness to Experience on Interracial Attitudes and Impression Formation. Journal of Personality and Social Psychology **88**(5), 816-826
[2]Heath, M., and Mulligan, E., (2007) Seeking open minded doctors – how women who identify as bisexual, queer or lesbian seek quality health care. Australian Family Physician **36**(6), 469-471

Attention and awareness

[1]A Harvard Health article, (2019) Benefits of Mindfulness [online] Available at: https://www.helpguide.org/harvard/benefits-of-mindfulness.htm [Accessed 16.4.20] and
Howell, A., J., *et al* (2008) Relations among mindfulness, well-being and sleep. Personality and Individual Differences **45**(8), 773-777
[2]Georgiou, M., (2015) Attention Span Crisis in our Schools. Synergy 13(1)
[3]Knapton, S., (2015) Mindfulness is stopping the world from thinking [online] Available at: https://www.telegraph.co.uk/culture/hay-festival/11629029/Mindfulness-is-stopping-the-world-from-thinking.html [Accessed 10.01.20]
[4]Cromwell, H., C., *et al* (2008) Sensory Gating: A

Translational Effort From Baisc to Clinical Science. Clincal EEG and Neuroscience **39**(2), 69-72

[5]Smith. K., (2008) Brains make decisions before you even know it [online] Available at: https://www.nature.com/news/2008/080411/full/news.2008.751.html [Accessed 10.02.20]

and

Soon.. C., S., *et al* (2008) Unconscious determinants of free decisions in the human brain. Nature Neuroscience **11**(5), 543-545

[6]Ohrnberger, J., Fichera, E., and Sutton, M., (2017) The relationship betwenn physical and mental heatlh: a mediation analysis. Social Science and Medicine **195**, 42-49

[7]Logie, K., and Frewen, P., (2015) Self/Other Referential Processing Following Mindfulness and Loving-Kindness Meditation.Mindfulness **6**, 778-787

and

Goldin, P., Ramel, W., and Gross, J., (2009) Mindfulness Meditation Training and Self-Referential Processing in Social Anxiety Disorder: Behavioural and Neural Effects. Journal of Cognitive Psychotherapy 23(3), 242-257

[8]Farb, N., *et al* (2013) Mindfulness meditation training alters cortical representations of interoceptive attention. Social Cognitive and Affective Neuroscience **8**(1), 15-26

and

Lazar, S., *et al* (2005) Meditation experience is associated with increased cortical thickness. Neuroreport **16**(17), 1893-1897

[9]Regan, D., (2020) How the challenging behaviour of a traumatised child tells their trauma story and is a vital part of their recovery. Journal of Social Work Practice **34**(1), 113-118

Allowing and accepting

[1]Chun, Shao-Hsi., et al (2012) The Impact of Cognitive Flexibility on Resistance to Organizational Change. Social Behaviour and Personality: an international journal **40**(5), 735-745

[2]Egbert, M., and Barandiaran, Xabier., (2014) Modeling habits as self-sustaining patterns or sensorimotor behavior. Frontiers in Human Neuroscience **8** 590

and

Graybiel, A., (2008) Habits, Rituals, and the Evaluative Brain. Annual Review of Neuroscience **31**(1), 359-387

[3]Mcnerney, S., (2013) Mindfulness: Observing Without Questioning [online] Available at: https://bigthink.com/insights-of-genius/the-perils-of-asking-ques-tions [Accessed 21.04.20]

[4]Golubickis, M., et al (2016) The observing self: Diminishing egocentrism through brief mindfulness meditation. European Journal of Social Psychology **46**(4) 521-527

[5]Epstein, S. (2003). Cognitive■Experiential Self■Theory of Personality. In Handbook of Psychology, I.B. Weiner (Ed.). doi:10.1002/0471264385.wei0507

[6]NHS (2018) Mindfulness [online] Available at: https://www.nhs.uk/conditions/stress-anxiety-depression/mindfulness/ [Accessed 21.4.20]

[7]Robson, D., (2019) A New Trial Of An Ancient Rhetorical

Trick Finds It Can Make You Wiser [online] Available
at: https://digest.bps.org.uk/2019/05/24/a-new-tri-
al-of-an-ancient-rhetorical-trick-finds-it-can-make-
you-wiser/ [Accessed 21.4.20]

[8]Ostafin, Brian., and Marlatt, Alan., (2008) Surfing the
Urge: Experiential Acceptance Moderates the
Relation Between Automatic Alcohol Motivation and
Hazardous Drinking. Journal of Social and Clinical
Psychology: **27**(4), 404-418

[9]Ackerman, C., (2020) 23 Amazing Health Benefits of
Mindfulness for Body and Brain [online] Available at:
https://positivepsychology.com/benefits-of-mindful-
ness/ [Accessed 22.04.20]

[10]Halliwell, E., (2014) Mindfulness Can't Cure Everything.
And That's a Problem Why? [online] Available at:
https://www.mindful.org/mindfulness-cant-cure-
everything-and-thats-a-problem-why/ [Accessed
22.4.20]

[11]Pickut, B., *et al* (2013) Mindfulness based intervention in Parkinson's disease leads to structural brain
changes on MRI: A randomized controlled longitudi-
nal trial. Clinical Neurology and Neurosurgery **115**(12),
2419-2425

and

Tang, Y., *et al* (2015) The neuroscience of mindfulness
meditation. Nature Reviews Neuroscience **16**, 213-225
(and also Erratum: 312)

and

Hölzel, B., *et al* (2011) Mindfulness practice leads to
increases in regional brain gray matter density.
Psychiatry Research: Neuroimaging **191**(1), 36-43

[12]Zadra, J., and Clore, G., (2011) Emotion and perception: the role of affective information. *Wiley Interdiscip Rev Cogn Sci.***1;2**(6), 676–685

[13]Cole, N., (2017) 15 Sad Reasons People Give Up On Their Dreams [online] Available at: https://www.inc.com/ nicolas-cole/15-sad-reasons-people-give-up-on-their-dreams.html [Accessed 22.4.20]

[14]Pillay, S., (2016) Greater self-acceptance improves emotional well-being [online] Available at: https:// www.health.harvard.edu/blog/greater-self-ac-ceptance-improves-emotional-well-201605169546 [Accessed 22.4.20]

[15]Morin, A., (2017) How to stop worrying about things you can't change [online] Available at: https://www. psychologytoday.com/gb/blog/what-mentally-strong-people-dont-do/201705/how-stop-worrying-about-things-you-cant-change and: https://www. forbes.com/sites/amymorin/2017/05/13/6-ways-to-stop-stressing-about-things-you-cant-control/ [accessed 22.4.20]

[16]Strauss, I., (2018) How to Deal With Family Members Who Stress You Out [online] Available at: https:// www.psychologytoday.com/us/blog/your-emotion-al-meter/201801/how-deal-family-members-who-stress-you-out [Accessed 22.4.20]

[17]Moreira, H., *et al* (2019) Editorial: Application of the Third Generation of Cognitive-Behavioral Approaches to Parenting [online] Available at: https://www.fron-tiersin.org/articles/10.3389/fpsyg.2019.02207/full [Accessed 22.04.20]

[18]Strazdins, L., and Loughrey B., (2007) Too busy: why

time is a health and environmental problem. NSW
Public Health Bulletin **18**, 219-221.

and

Pelletier, J., and Laska, M., (2012) Balancing Healthy Meals
and Busy Lives: Associations between Work, School,
and Family Responsibilities and Perceived Time
Constraints among Young Adults. Journal of Nutrition
Education and Behavior **44**(6), 481-489

[19]Nhat Hanh, T., (2001) 'Transformation' in *anger Buddhist
wisdom for cooling the flames*. Rider, pp. 67-88

and

Williams, M., and Penman, D., (2011) *Mindfulness a practical guide to FINDING PEACE IN A FRANTIC WORLD*.
Piatkus

Getting some practice started

[1]Segal, Z., Williams, M., and Teasdale, J., (2013) 'Gathering
the scattered mind' in *Mindfulness-Based Cognitive
Therapy for Depression* (2nd Ed.) The Guilford Press,
pp. 177-213

[2]Bien, T., (2006) *Mindful Therapy A Guide for Therapists
and Helping Professionals*. Wisdom Publications, pp.
54

[3]Maguire, H., (2015) Choosing and using your anchor in
meditation [online] Available at: http://so-mindful.
co.uk/benefits-of-mindfulness/choosing-and-us-
ing-your-anchor-in-meditation/ [Accessed 22.4.20]

[4]Nhat Hanh, T., (2012) *FEAR Essential Wisdom for Getting
Through the Storm*. Rider, pp. 85

[5]Gotink, R., *et al* (2016) 8-week Mindfulness Based Stress
Reduction induces brain changes similar to traditional

long-term meditation practice – A systematic review. Brain and Cognition **108**, 32-41

[6]Verni, K., (2015) *PRACTICAL MINDFULNESS A step-by-step guide*. DK London, pp. 6-13

[7]Mooji (2018) *Vaster Than Sky, Greater Than Space*. Coronet, pp. 20-24

[8]Kabat-Zinn, J., (2013) *FULL CATASTROPHE LIVING How to cope with stress, pain and illness using mindfulness meditation*. Piatkus, pp. 13

[9]Pert, C., (1997) *MOLECULES of EMOTION WHY YOU FEEL THE WAY YOU FEEL*. Simon and Schuster, pp. 140-149, 187

[10]Gray, K., *et al* (2011) More than a body: Mind perception and the nature of objectification. Journal of Personality and Social Psychology, **101**(6), 1207-1220

[11]James 4:17, Holy Bible: King James Version

Acknowledging and advancing

[1]Hawks, S., (2013) Spiritual Wellness, Holistic Health, and the Practice of Health Education. American Journal of Health Education, **35**(1), 11-18

[2]Integrating Mental & Physical healthcare: Research, Training & Services (IMPARTS)(2013) Understanding the mind-body link [online] Available at: https://www.kcl.ac.uk/ioppn/depts/pm/research/imparts/Quick-links/Self-Help-Materials/Mind-Body-Link.pdf [Accessed 29.4.20]

[3]Collard, P., (2013) *Mindfulness-Based Cognitive Therapy FOR DUMMIES*. John Wiley & Sons Ltd, pp. 77-97

[4]Mindvalley (2018) Subconscious Definition: The Hidden Power of Your Mind [online] Available at: https://blog.

mindvalley.com/subconscious-definition/ [Accessed 23.4.20]

[5]Baldelomar, R., (2017) Manage Your Mental Energy To Be More Productive At Work [online] Available at: https://www.forbes.com/sites/raquelbaldelomar/2017/01/31/manage-your-mental-energy-to-be-more-productive-at-work/ [Accessed 23.4.20]
and
Amir, O., (2008) Tough Choices: How Making Decisions Tires Your Brain [online] Available at:https://www.scientificamerican.com/article/tough-choices-how-making/ [Accessed 23.4.20]

[6]Fox, D., et al (2007) Intrinsic Fluctuations within Cortical Systems Account for Intertrial Variability in Human Behaviour. Neuron, **56**(1), 171-184

[7]Chan, D., (2016) Learning to see things from another's perspective [online] Available at: https://www.strait-stimes.com/opinion/learning-to-see-things-from-anothers-perspective [Accessed 22.4.20]

[8]Lebow, J., and Stroud, C., (2012) Assessment of effective couple and family functioning: Prevailing models and instruments. In F. Walsh (Ed.), *Normal family processes: Growing diversity and complexity* (p. 501–528). The Guilford Press.

[9]Jackson, B., (2017) Connection Before Correction [online] Available at: https://raisereadykids.com/connection-before-correction/ [Accessed 23.3.20]

[10]Robbins, R., (2001) *AWAKEN THE GIANT WITHIN*. Simon and Schuster, pp. 123-150

[11]Morsella, E., and Poehlman, T., (2013) The inevitable contrast: Conscious vs. Unconscious processes in action

control. Frontiers in Psychology, **4**, 590

[12]Goleman, D., (2017) 'Resilience for the Rest of Us' in *Emotional Intelliegnce RESILIENCE*. Harvard Business School, pp. 31-38

[13]HelpGuide (2020) Improving Family Relationships with Emotional Intelligence [online] Available at: https://www.helpguide.org/articles/mental-health/improving-family-relationships-with-emotional-intelligence.htm [Accessed 23.4.20]

[14]Weare, K., (2013), Developing mindfulness with children and young people: a review of the evidence and policy context. Journal of Children's Services, **8**(2), 141-153

and

Langer, E., (2011) 'Mindfulness Versus Positive Evaluation' in *The Oxford Handbook of Positive Psychology*. Oxford University Press, pp .279-294

and

Garland, E., *et al* (2009) The Role of Mindfulness in Positive Reappraisal. Explore, **5**(1), 37-44

[15]Grecucci, A., *et al* (2015) Mindful Emotion Regulation: Exploring the Neurocognitive Mechanisms behind Mindfulness. Psychological Effects of Mind and Body Practices, (review paper)

[16]'Mindfulness.' *The Mind, Explained*. (2019). Netflix

[17]Salzberg, S., (2013) Mindfulness and Difficult Emotions [online] Available at: *https://tricycle.org/magazine/mindfulness-and-difficult-emotions/* [accessed 24.4.20]

[18]Dass, R., (2015) Meditation and Expectations [online] Available at: *https://www.ramdass.org/meditate-expectations/* [Accessed 24.4.20]

[19]Stillman, J., (2017) Finding Meaning in Life Is Way Easier

Than You Think, Happy New Science Shows [online]
Available at: https://www.inc.com/jessica-stillman/
youre-life-is-already-way-more-meaningful-than-you.
html [Accessed 24.4.20]

[20]Bechtle, M., (2012) PEOPLE CAN'T DRIVE YOU CRAZY IF
YOU DON'T GIVE THEM THE KEYS. Revell, pp. 31-41,
51-67

[21]Court, J., (2017) Active Listening Skills for Today's
Family [online] Available at: https://volumeone.org/
news/2017/03/24/16998_active_listening_skills_for_
todays_family [Accessed 24.4.20]

[22]Deschene, L., (2010) How to Deal with Criticism Well: 25
Reasons to Embrace It [online] Available at:https://
tinybuddha.com/blog/how-to-deal-with-criticism-well-
25-reasons-to-embrace-it/ [Accessed 24.4.20]

[23]Tolle, E., (2011) THE POWER OF NOW A Guide to Spiritual
Enlightenment. Hodder and Stoughton Ltd, pp. 27-38

[24]Mystics of India (2018) Sadhguru's 5 Rules of Love and
Relationships. [online video] Availble at: https://
www.youtube.com/watch?v=s-d0uEChXRE [accessed
24.4.20]

[25]Rasheed, A., (2018) Will Smith Explains Why It's Not
His Responsibility To Make His Wife Happy [online]
Available at: https://hauteliving.com/2018/02/will-
smith-jada-pinkett-smith/651889/ [Accessed 24.4.20]
and
Turner, E., (2018) Your Partner Is Not Responsible For Your
Happiness [online] Available at: https://psiloveyou.xyz/
your-partner-is-not-responsible-for-your-happiness-
2fc88fb29bec [Accessed 24.4.20]

[26]Wolkin, J., (2015) Cultivating multiple aspects of

attention through mindfulness meditation accounts for psychological well-being through decreased rumination. Psychology Research and Behavior Management, **8**, 171-180

[27]Marshall, J., (2015) *Managing Anxiety with Mindfulness FOR DUMMIES*. John Wiley & Sons Ltd, pp. 7-20

[28]Rampton, J., (2017) 4 Proven Ways to Deal With Stress Without Shutting Down, Giving Up or Taking Meds [online] Available at: *https://www.entrepreneur.com/ article/299225* [Accessed 24.4.20]

[29]Arnsten, A., *et al* (2012) Neural circuits responsible for self-control are highly vulnerable to even mild stress. When they shut down, primal impulses go unchecked and mental paralysis sets in. Scientific American, **306**(4), 48-53

[30]Markham, L., (2012) *Peaceful Parent, HAPPY KIDS How to Stop Yelling and Start Connecting*. Perigee, pp. 1-35

[31]Snyder, C., (2019) *Episode 88 – "Do As I Say Not As I Do" Never Works*. [Podcast] 24 January. Available at: *https://baandek.org/posts/do-as-i-say-not-as-i-do-never-works/* and *https://podcasts.apple.com/us/ podcast/episode-88-do-as-i-say-not-as-i-do-nev-er-works/id1156938377?i=1000428363341* (Accessed 24.4.20)

[32]Diaz, L., (2017) The Ultimate Form of Human Connection: Sharing Our Weaknesses [online] Available at: *https://byrslf.co/the-ultimate-form-of-hu-man-connection-sharing-our-weaknesses-f26da97f-c7d6* [Accessed 24.4.20]

[33]Rinpoche, Y., (2009) *THE JOY OF LIVING UNLOCKING THE SECRETS AND SCIENCE OF* HAPPINESS. Random

House Group, pp.147

[34]Gyatso, K., (2002) *Transform your life A Blissful Journey* Tharpa Publications, pp. 97-114

[35]Sanders, S., Families and households in the UK 2019 [online] Available at: *https://www.ons.gov.uk/peoplepopulationandcommunity/birthsdeathsandmarriages/families/bulletins/familiesandhouseholds/2019* [Accessed 25.4.20]

[36]Le Fanu, J., (1999) *OVERCOMING ANXEITY A self-help guide using Cognitive Behavioural Techniques.* Robinson Publishing Ltd, pp. 100-111

[37]Vishen Lakhiana (2018) Your Children Are Not Your Own [online video] Availble at: https://youtu.be/gsb8RGkoxEY [accessed 14.3.20]

[38]Bealing, J., (2015) Family stability, not family structure, is key to education success, says Sussex study. [online] Available at: *http://www.sussex.ac.uk/broadcast/read/29675* [Accessed 12.1.20]

[39]Gyatso, K., (2005) *How to Solve Our Human Problems The Four Noble Truths.* Tharpa Publications, pp. Viii-x

Appreciation

[1]Wong, J., and Brown, J., (2017) How Gratitude Changes You and Your Brain [online] Available at: *https://greatergood.berkeley.edu/article/item/how_gratitude_changes_you_and_your_brain* [Accessed 3.4.20]

[2]Toepfer, S., *et al* (2012) Letters of Gratitude: Further Evidence for Author Benefits. Journal of Happiness Studies, **13**, 187-201
and
Morin, A., (2014) Benefits Of Gratitude That Will Motivate

You To Give Thanks Year-Round [online] Available at: *https://www.forbes.com/sites/amymorin/2014/11/23/7-scientifically-proven-benefits-of-gratitude-that-will-motivate-you-to-give-thanks-year-round/* [Accessed 2.2.20]

and

Emmons, R., et al (2019) 'Gratitude' in *M. W. Gallagher & S. J. Lopez, Positive psychological assessment: A handbook of models and measures.* American Psychological Association pp. 317-332.

[3]Visuddhācāra, (2000) *DRINKING TEA LIVING LIFE Applying Mindfulness In Everyday Life and Critical Times.* C.W.Printing

[4]Cutler, C., and HH Dalai Lama, (1999) *The Art of Happiness.* Hodder and Stoughton, pp. 1-11

[5]Wood, A., et al (2010) Gratitude and well-being: A review and theroetical integration. Clinical Psychology Review, **30**(7), 890-905

[6]HH The Dalai Lama (2004) *THE MANY WAYS TO NIRVANA.* Hodder and Staughton, pp. 41-67

[7]HH The Dalai Lama., (2002) *AN OPEN HEART PRACTISING COMPASSION IN EVERYDAY LIFE.* Hodder and Staughton, pp. 75-80

[8]Tolle, E., (2018) 2 July. Availalbe at: *https://twitter.com/eckharttolle/status/1013673121830842369?lang=en* [Accessed 12.12.2019]

[9]Peters, S., (2012) *The Chimp Paradox.* Vermilion, pp. 293-316

[10]HH Dalai Lama., (2008) *THE UNIVERSE IN A SINGLE ATOM.* Abacus, pp. 127-146

[11]McCraty, R., and Childre, D., (2004) 'The Grateful Heart' in

The *Psychology of Gratitude*. Oxford University Press,
pp. 231-235

[12]Calvin, W., (1997) *HOW BRAINS THINK*. Harper Collins, pp.
136 and 140

[13]Carlson, L., *et al* (2007) One year pre-post intervention
follow-up of psychological, immune, endocrine and
blood pressure outcomes of mindfulness-based
stress reduction (MBSR) in breast and prostate can-
cer outpatients. Brain, Behavior and Immunity, **21**(8),
1038-1049

[14]Carmody, J., and Baer, R., (2008) Relationships between
mindfulness practice and levels of mindfulness,
medical and psychological symptoms and well-being
in a mindfulness-based stress reduction program.
Journal of Behavioral Medicine, **31**, 23-33

[15]Greeson, J., and Brantley, J., (2009) 'Mindfulness and
Anxiety Disorders: Developing a Wise Relationship
with the Inner Experience of Fear' in *Clinical
Handbook of Mindfulness*. Springer, pp. 171-188

[16]Teasdale, J., *et al* (2000) Prevention of relapse/recur-
rence in major depression by mindfulness-based
cognitive therapy. Journal of Consulting and Clinical
Psychology, **68**(4), 615-623

[17]de Castro, J., (2018) The Noble Eightfold Path: Right
Effort [online] Available at: *http://contemplative-stud-
ies.org/wp/index.php/2018/03/04/the-noble-eightfold-
path-right-effort-2/* [Accessed 27.4.20]

Obstacles to establishing practice

[1]Fronsdal, G., (2004) Doubting Doubt: Practicing With
the Final Hindrance [online] Available at: *https://*

www.insightmeditationcenter.org/books-articles/
the-five-hindrances-handouts/doubting-doubt-prac-
ticing-with-the-final-hindrance/ [Accessed 27.2.20]
[2]Kornfield, J., (2020) Obstacles Are Part of the Path
[online] Available at: https://jackkornfield.com/mak-
ing-the-hindrances-part-of-the-path/ [Accessed
25.2.20]
[3]Kahneman, D., (2012) Thinking, Fast and Slow. Pengiun
Books, pp. 19-30
[4]Thompson, B., (2015) your thoughts are like a hitchhiker,
desperately wanting for you to stop and pick them
up [online] Available at: http://www.zenthinking.net/
blog/2015/4/6/your-thoughts-are-like-a-hitchhiker
[Accessed 27.4.20]
[5]Gladwell, M., (2005) Blink: The Power of Thinking Without
Thinking. Penguin Books, pp. 99-146.
[6]TEDx Talks (2018) How to stop your thoughts from controlling your life [online video] Available at: https://
www.youtube.com/watch?v=29Vj0-TVHiQ [Accessed
12.1.20]
[7]Coxon, M., (2011) New voices: The problem with rumination [online] Available at: https://thepsychologist.bps.
org.uk/volume-24/edition-1/new-voices-problem-rumi-
nation [Accessed 27.4.20]
[8]Gale, M., (2018) How Busy Working Parents Can Make
Time for Mindfulness [online] Available at: https://
www.mindful.org/busy-working-parents-can-make-
time-mindfulness/ [Accessed 12.12.19]
[9]Goldstein, E., and Goldstein, S., (2016) Raising the Mindful
Family [online] Available at: https://www.mindful.org/
raising-the-mindful-family/ [Accessed 12.12.19]

Affection

[1]Ricard, M., (2016) Altruism THE POWER OF COMPASSION TO CHANGE YOURSELF AND THE WORLD. Back Bay Books, pp. 24

[2]Rinpoche, S., (1992) THE TIBETAN BOOK OF LIVING AND DYING. Rider Books, pp 187-208

[3]Borg, J., (2010) Mind Power Change your Thinking Change Your Life. Pearson Education Ltd, pp. 35-66

[4]Lama Surya Das, (1999) Awakening to the Sacred. Broadway Books, pp. 321-318

[5]HH Dalai Lama, and Chan, V., (2012) THE WISDOM OF COMPASSION. Riverhead Books, pp. lx-x

[6]Morgan. C., (2020) Leanr the Different Types of Love (and Better Understand Your Partner) [online] Availalbe at: https://www.lifehack.org/816195/types-of-love [Accessed 27.4.20]

[7]Neff, K., and Germer, C., (2019) The Transformative Effects of Mindful Self-Compassion [online] Available at: https://www.mindful.org/the-transformative-effects-of-mindful-self-compassion/ [Accessed: 27.4.20]

[8]Lama Surya Das, (1997) Awakening the Buddha Within. Broadway Books, pp. 101

[9]Watt, D., (2019) The Link Between Judging and Compassion [online] Available at: https://theyogaconnection.me/the-link-between-judging-and-compassion/ [Accessed 21.11.19]

[10]Witchalls, C., (2011) Why a lack of empathy is the root of all evil [online] Available at: https://www.independent.co.uk/life-style/health-and-families/

features/why-a-lack-of-empathy-is-the-root-of-all-evil-6279239.html [Accessed 21.11.19]

[11]Kanchanalak. P., (2011) Searching for the fourth monkey in a corrupted world [online] Available at: *https://web.archive.org/web/20150828032149/http://www.nation-multimedia.com/home/2011/04/21/opinion/Searching-for-the-fourth-monkey-in-a-corrupted-wor-30153534.html* [Accessed 27.4.20]

and

Wikipedia (20200 Three wise monkeys [online] Available at: *https://en.wikipedia.org/wiki/Three_wise_monkeys* [Accessed 27.4.20]

[12]Cambridge Dictionary (2020) empathy [online] Available at: *https://dictionary.cambridge.org/dictionary/english/empathy* [Accessed 27.4.20]

[13]Jones, S., *et al* (2016) The Impact of Mindfulness on Empathy, Active Listening, and Perceived Provisions of Emotional Support. Communication Research, **46**(6), 838-865

and

Kemper, K., and Khirallah, M., (2015) Acute Effects of Online Mind-Body Skills Training on Resilience, Mindfulness, and Empathy. Journal of Evidence-Based Integrative Medicine, **20**(4), 247-53

[14]Robson, D., (2017) A new way to look at emotions – and how to master yours [online] Available at: *https://www.bbc.com/future/article/20171012-how-emotions-can-trick-your-mind-and-body* [Accessed 25.11.19]

[15]Singer, M., (2007) The untethered soul the journey beyond yourself. Noetic Books, pp. 23-29

[16]Weisman, O., *et al* (2012) Oxytocin Administration to

Parents Enhances Infant Physiological and Behavioral Readiness for Social Engagement. Biological Psychiatry, **72**(12), 982-989

[17]Abraham, E., and Hendler, T., (2014) Father's brain is sensitive to childcare experiences. Psychological and Cognitive Sciences, **111**(27), 9792-9797

and

Dockterman, E., (2014) Gay Dad's Brains Develop Just Like Those of Straight Parents, Study Finds [online] Available at: *https://time.com/116843/gay-dads-brains-develop-just-like-those-of-straight-parents-study-finds/* [Accessed November 2019]

[18]Petersson, M., *et al* (2017) Oxytocin and Cortisol Levels in Dog Owners and Their Dogs Are Associated with Behavioral Patterns: An Exploratory Study. Frontiers in Psychology, **8**,17986

[19]Machida, S., *et al* (2018) Oxytocin Release during the Meditation of Altruism and Appreciation (Arigato-Zen). International Journal of Neurology Research, **4(1),** 364-370

[20]BBC News (2017) Marvyn Iheanacho jailed for killing boy over lost trainer [online] Available at: *https://www.bbc.co.uk/news/uk-england-london-40716286* [Accessed 27.4.20]

[21]Humanity in Action (2011) Reflections on the Holocaust. Humanity in Action, pp. 37

[22]Resnick, B., (2017) A psychologist explains the limits of human compassion [online] Available at: *https://www.vox.com/explainers/2017/7/19/15925506/psychic-numbing-paul-slovic-apathy* [Accessed 28.4.20]

Associating and aiming

[1]NHS, (2016) Exercise in middle-age 'stops your brain shrinking' [online] Available at: *https://www.nhs.uk/news/lifestyle-and-exercise/exercise-in-middle-age-stops-your-brain-shrinking/* [Accessed 10.12.19]
and
Foley, K., (2019) How the human brain stays young even as we age [online] Available at: *https://qz.com/1708872/the-human-brain-is-the-most-resilient-organ-in-the-body/* [Accessed 10.12.19]
and
Hillman, C., *et al* (2014) Effects of the FITKids Randomized Controlled Trial on Executive Control and Brain Function. Pediatrics, **134**(4), 2013-3219
[2]Alda, M., *et al* (2016) Zen meditation, Length of Telomeres, and the Role of Experiential Avoidance and Compassion. Mindfulness, **7**, 651-659
and
Hoge, E., *et al* (2013) Loving-Kindness Meditation practice associated with longer telomeres in women. Brain, Behavior, and Immunity, **32**, 159-163
[3]Berliet, M., (2016) Love won't fix your life, so stop expecting it to [online] Available at: *https://thoughtcatalog.com/melanie-berliet/2016/02/love-wont-fix-your-life-so-stop-expecting-it-to/* [Accessed 20.2.20]
and
Efap, S., (2013) Don't Expect, Earn Respect [online] Available at: *https://www.elitedaily.com/life/motivation/expect-earn-respect* [Accessed 20.2.20]
and

Picicci, J., (2019) How Expectations Undermine Our Relationships and Happiness [online] Available at: https://tinybuddha.com/blog/how-expectations-undermine-our-relationships-and-happiness/ [Accessed 20.2.20]

[4]Wiebe, J., (2018) What is Catastrophic Thinking? (And How to Stop) [online] Available at: https://www.talkspace.com/blog/catastrophic-thinking-thought-spirals-how-to-stop/ [Accessed 28.4.20]

[5]Wikipedia (2020) Desiderata [online] Available at: https://en.wikipedia.org/wiki/Desiderata [Accessed 28.4.20]

[6]Team Tony (2020) WHAT MOTIVATES YOU TO TAKE ACTION? [online] Available at: https://www.tonyrobbins.com/productivity-performance/what-motivates-you-to-take-action/ [Accessed 28.4.20]

[7]Brasington, L., (2015) Right Concentration A Practical Guide to the Jhānas. Shambala Publications, pp. 68-74

[8]Wikipedia (2020) Maslow's Heirarchy of Needs [ONLINE] Available at: https://en.wikipedia.org/wiki/Maslow%27s_hierarchy_of_needs [Accessed 09.11.20]

[9]Servan-Schreiber, D., (2005) healing without freud or prozac. Rodale International, pp.171-173

[10]Crofford, L., (2015) Chronic Pain: Where the Body Meets the Brain. Transactions of the American Clinical and Climatological Association, **126**, 167-183

and

Jeffs, A., (2019) Suffering is in your mind... [online] Available at: https://thriveglobal.com/stories/suffering-is-in-your-mind/ [Accessed 28.4.20] and

Martinez-Calderon, J., (2018) The role of psychological factors in the perpetuation of pain intensity and disability in people with chronic shoulder pain: a systematic review. Rehabilitation medicine research, **8**(4),

[11]Fremantle, F., (2017) What Turns the Wheel of Life [online] Available at: *https://www.lionsroar.com/what-turns-the-wheel-of-life/* [Accessed 29.4.20]

[12]Alux.com (2018) 15 Things You CAN'T Control In Life [online video] Available at: https://youtu.be/p5ST2Db-PGpY [Accessed 29.4.20]

AND

TEDxTalks (2017) From Clutter to Clarity [online video] Available at: *https://www.youtube.com/watch?v=Crs-doIOGCRw* [Accessed 29.4.20]

[13]Abhayagiri Buddhist Monastery (2017) Understanding Conditioning of the Mind [online video] Available at: *https://www.youtube.com/watch?v=ONtHedq4NnQ* [Accessed 29.4.20]

[14]Ziglar, Z., (2002) Goals [Audio CD] Nightingale-Conant, CD1 Track 2

[15]Robbins, A., (MP3) Stop Yourself From Financial Self Sabotage, 01 of 07

[16]Rinpoche, S., (MP3) Turning Suffering & Happiness into Enlightenment, 7.1 'it's extremely difficult'

[17]Powers, A., (2018) Failing Your Way To Success: Why Failure Is A Crucial Ingredient For Success [online] Available at: *https://www.forbes.com/sites/annapowers/2018/04/30/failing-your-way-to-success-why-failure-is-a-crucial-ingredient-for-success/* [Accessed 29.04.20]

[18]Goldhill, O., (2015) Neuroscience backs up the Buddhist belief that "the self" isn't constant, but ever-changing [online] Available at: *https://qz.com/506229/neuroscience-backs-up-the-buddhist-belief-that-the-self-isnt-constant-but-ever-changing/* [Accessed 29.4.20]
[19]Dedyukhina, A., (2017) How Much Is Your Attention Worth? [online] Available at: *https://workforceinstitute.org/how-much-is-your-attention-worth/* [Accessed 29.4.20]

Printed in Great Britain
by Amazon